EDUCATION in America

APRIL GRAZIANO

Cover image © Shutterstock.com

www.kendallhunt.com
Send all inquiries to:
4050 Westmark Drive
Dubuque, IA 52004-1840

Copyright © 2020 by Kendall Hunt Publishing Company

ISBN 978-1-7924-3701-4

All rights reserved. No part of this publication may be reproduced,
stored in a retrieval system, or transmitted, in any form or by any means,
electronic, mechanical, photocopying, recording, or otherwise,
without the prior written permission of the copyright owner.

Published in the United States of America

A great teacher makes connections with students beyond the curriculum. A great teacher is not only is knowledgeable and skillful, but also *inspires* students.

Dedication

To my parents, Jim and Sandy MacDonald, who were my first teachers. To my daughters, Andrea and Julia, who have listened to my teaching stories for over 20 years.

CONTENTS

Features. .... *ix*
Student Contributors .... *xi*
Objectives Addressed in Education in America................................. *xiii*
List of Graphs and Charts .... *xv*

Section I The Field of Education **1**
    Chapter 1   Educational Philosophies 3
    Chapter 2   Educational Organizations 15

Section II Quality Educators **35**
    Chapter 3   Art & Science 37
    Chapter 4   Highly Qualified..47
    Chapter 5   Teacher & Student Diversity 63
    Chapter 6   Benefits & Challenges of Teaching 95

Section III Teaching & Learning **111**
    Chapter 7   Pedagogy & Learning Environments.....................113
    Chapter 8   Curriculum & Assessment.....................................123

Appendices **131**
    Appendix 1   Bibliography...133
    Appendix 2   Additional Field Experience Forms 135
    Appendix 3   Additional Worksheets & Assignments................145

Glossary *161*

FEATURES

Student Voices

I absolutely love teaching community college students. There is a richness of diversity in students' work experiences, backgrounds, and demographics that encourages a deeper level of classroom discussion. As I reviewed assignments and final grades from my spring 2020 courses, I was very proud of what my students accomplished, especially given the extreme difficulties we all faced during the semester. I kept finding myself wishing I could include the ideas they expressed from learning about American education, and I'm happy to be able to include a few representations of their ideas as Student Voices features in each section and chapter.

Media Extensions

There is a wealth of information available in video and other media formats that help bring topics to life. Being able to see and hear content that supports textbook chapters can help students learn about education from different formats and approaches in Media Extensions. I've included this feature at least once in each chapter, and this is a great way for students who are interested in a topic to be able to learn more.

Field Experience Documents

Observing classrooms is a key factor in helping determine whether or not someone wants to teach, and at which level or area they want to teach. Field experience documents, including documentation forms for school or childcare visits, interview forms, and reflection papers, will help students record their efforts to learn about the field of education. These are included early in the textbook so students can prepare for these experiences. Additional copies are included in the appendices.

Chapter Worksheets

Each chapter has worksheets for reflection and for continued exploration of topics. These print and electronic assignments are designed to help students and faculty consider the field of education from a variety of perspectives. Additional blank copies of the worksheets are available in the appendices.

STUDENT CONTRIBUTORS

Special thanks go to students who have given me permission to include their views in Student Voices.

Faith Ballard
Abegail Brown
Jovanni Camacho
Joshua Cook
Marissa Mansfield
Samantha Montanez
Ron Montgomery

Reagan Os
Patrick Olszewski

Hannah Roberts
Mikayla Scott
Gia Sellica
Pandora Washburn

OBJECTIVES ADDRESSED IN EDUCATION IN AMERICA

	S1 The Field of Education		S2 Quality Educators				S3 Teaching and Learning	
	C1 Educational Philosophies	C2 Educational Organizations	C3 Art and Science of Teaching	C4 Highly Qualified	C5 Teacher and Student Diversity	C6 Benefits and Challenges of Teaching	C7 Pedagogy and Learning Environments	C8 Curriculum and Assessment
1. Communicate effectively with educational terms	X	X	X	X	X	X	X	X
2. Interpret data presented in graphs and charts about the field of education	X	X	X	X	X	X	X	
3. Explore the nature and value of education in society	X	X				X		X
4. Demonstrate an understanding of education from historical, philosophical, social, and political frameworks	X	X	X		X	X		X
5. Explore the role of schools in maintaining, perpetuating, and influencing culture, both nationally and internationally	X		X		X		X	X
6. Develop knowledgeable, reflective, and critical perspectives of education	X	X	X	X	X	X	X	X
7. Debate current standards, requirements, and trends in early childhood through secondary education	X	X	X	X	X	X	X	X
8. Identify the degree to which one's strengths and interests are consistent with the demands of teaching and related professions	X			X				

LIST OF GRAPHS and CHARTS

Figure 1.1	Traditional Educational Philosophies	4
Figure 1.2	Progressive Educational Philosophies	5
Figure 1.3	Increasing Student Roles in Learning	6
Figure 2.1	Common Characteristics of Four Types of Schooling	16
Figure 2.2	School Administration	18
Figure 2.3	Degrees in Higher Education	19
Figure 2.4	Examples of Academic Organizations for Educators	20
Figure 3.1	Examples of Teaching Skills	38
Figure 3.2	Average Public School Class Size, 2017 to 2018	39
Figure 4.1	Racial/Ethnic Backgrounds of Public and Private School Teachers	48
Figure 4.2	Highest Academic Degrees Held by Public and Private School Teachers, 2017 to 2018	49
Figure 4.3	Graduate or Undergraduate Coursework Prior to First Year of Teaching	50
Figure 4.4	State Preschool Standards and Teacher Qualifications 2016 to 2017	50
Figure 4.5	Test Required for Initial Teacher Certification of Elementary and Secondary Teachers	53
Figure 4.6	Positive Impact of Evaluation on Teaching	56
Figure 5.1	Reasons Why Hiring Efforts Alone Are Not Enough	65
Figure 5.2	Possible Ways to Increase Teacher Diversity	65
Figure 5.3	Representing Culturally Responsive Pedagogy in the Classroom	91
Figure 6.1	Average Base Salaries of Public and Private School Teachers, 2017 to 2018	96
Figure 6.2	Negotiated Agreement Salary Scale	97
Figure 6.3	Comparison of Average Annual Salaries—Teachers and U.S. Average for All Jobs	98
Figure 6.4	Top Five Average Teacher Salaries in the United States	99
Figure 6.5	Areas of U.S. Teacher Autonomy	100
Figure 6.6	Sources of Stress for Teachers	101
Figure 7.1	Common Teaching Methods	113
Figure 7.2	Selecting and Adjusting Teaching Methods	114
Figure 7.3	Examples of Traditional and Progressive Classrooms	116

SECTION I
The Field of Education

> **STUDENT VOICES**
>
> "Education is an important aspect of human life. From learning how to read and write to learning how to be an active member of society, education is at the heart of it all. But before we can have successful students, we need successful teachers."

Chapters

1. Educational Philosophies   3
2. Educational Organizations   15

Current Issues and Trends to Be Explored

Charter Schools
Class Size
Educational Funding
Failing Schools
Mandated Schooling
Student-Centered Teaching
Turn-around Plans
Universal Preschool

CHAPTER 1
Educational Philosophies

STUDENT VOICES

For students to be able to find their interests, the educator needs to take a step back and let the students have a role in building the curriculum. Teachers should be trained in how to let the students take control, while still guiding them in learning the material they need to be successful.

Vocabulary

Educational Philosophy
Highly Qualified
Student-Centered
Teacher-Centered
Traditional Philosophies
Progressive Philosophies

Five Educational Philosophies

Essentialism
Perennialism
Progressivism
Social Reconstructionism
Existentialism

Objectives

1. Communicate effectively with educational terms
2. Interpret data presented in graphs and charts about the field of education
3. Explore the nature and value of education in society
4. Demonstrate an understanding of education from historical, philosophical, social, and political frameworks
5. Explore the role of schools in maintaining, perpetuating, and influencing culture, both nationally and internationally
6. Develop knowledgeable, reflective, and critical perspectives of education
7. Debate current standards, requirements, and trends in early childhood through secondary education
8. Identify the degree to which one's strengths and interests are consistent with the demands of teaching and related professions

Educational Philosophy

How teachers teach and the ways they help students learn vary greatly from one teacher to another. Why does one teacher have students in rows and have them work in pairs? Why does another teacher have students choose their own topics to study? Why teachers do what they do is based on their **educational philosophy**. Philosophy is a system of thought or perspective, and educational philosophy refers to what someone thinks about teaching and learning, including what the teacher-student-community roles are and what content should be studied.

> **Educational philosophy**– A system of thought about teaching and learning

3

Traditional Philosophy

There are two traditional philosophies of American education, which are shown in Figure 1.1. They are called traditional because they are the first philosophies that people held about education in our country, but American education isn't very old because America is a relatively new country.

The first educational philosophy was **essentialism**, because it focused on the essential knowledge that a person needed to be a responsible member of society, and remembering the word "essential" can help you remember this educational philosophy. It was very teacher-centered and was common in colonial schools and early American classrooms. The teacher largely lectured or listened to students recite their lessons from memory. The material that was studied was focused on the basics: reading, writing, and math.

The next educational philosophy was **perennialism**. The word "perennial" can help you remember this, because something is perennial if it lasts over time. Teachers taught the basics, along with the ideas that have stood the test of time: languages, Shakespeare, the Bible, and documents such as the Magna Carta and the Constitution. Most of the content represented European thought, but it also included ideas from many ethnic groups from Asia and Africa, and contemporary and ancient cultures.

Figure 1.1 Traditional Educational Philosophies

Essentialism—Traditional
- Teacher-centered
- Focuses on essential ideas
- Preset curriculum with basics: reading, writing, math, Latin, and other languages

Perennialism—Traditional
- Teacher-centered
- Focuses on ideas that have stood the test of time
- Preset curriculum of classic literature, classic law, ideas from the Bible, ancient culture, Greek and Roman philosophy, etc.

Source: April Graziano

Progressive Philosophies

There are three progressive philosophies, which are shown in Figure 1.2: progressivism, social reconstructionism, and existentialism. **Progressivism** refers to the philosophical approach promoted by John Dewey, and American educator and philosopher who was instrumental in helping students have an active role in their learning. Progressivism focuses on the content that students need to become responsible citizens in American democracy. Rather than being passive listeners, students are expected to be actively involved in learning. They learn content as well as critical thinking skills. Since it was the first nontraditional educational philosophy, it is called progressivism. However, the educational philosophies that came after this theory are all progressive because they are student-centered instead of teacher-centered.

Social reconstructionism is student-centered, but it is focused on solving social issues through schools. Students learn about problems in society and try to find solutions for them. The teachers act as guides or facilitators, and students help determine the topics that they will study. The word "reconstruct" can help you remember that students are actively learning about fixing problems.

Existentialism is the most progressive educational philosophy. It is focused on existential questions, and the word "exist" can help you remember this philosophy. Not only is it student-centered and students choose the curriculum, but they also sometimes choose their own teachers to assist them with their learning projects.

Figure 1.2 Progressive Educational Philosophies

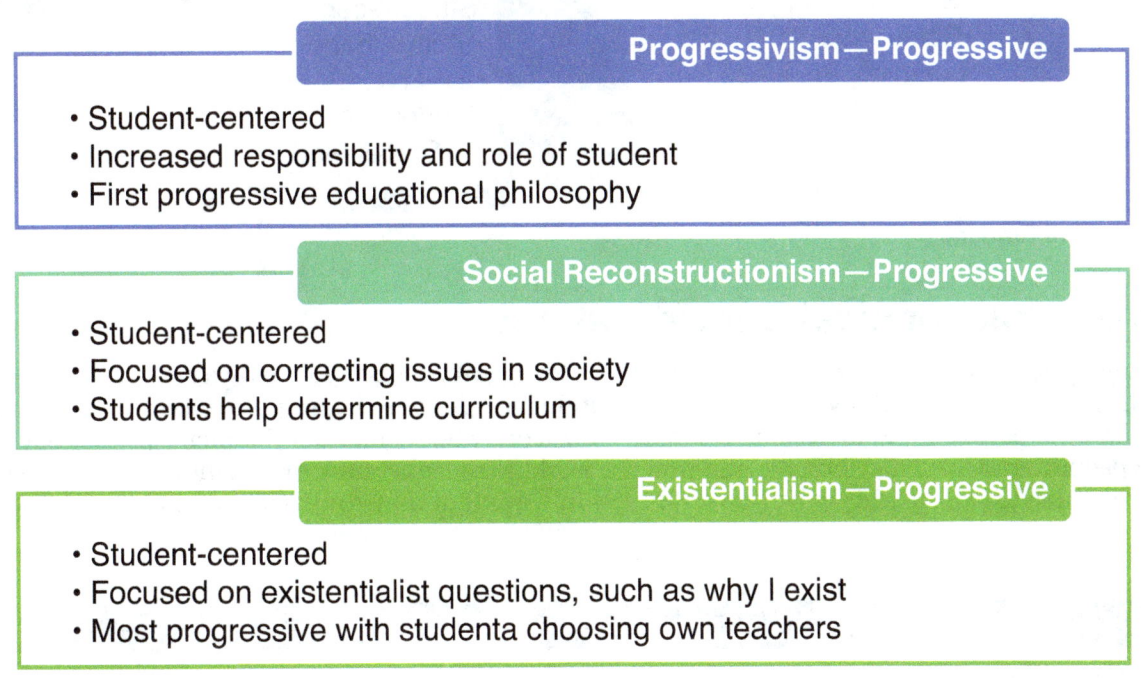

Source: April Graziano

Teacher and Student Roles

The biggest difference in these five educational philosophies are the roles of the students and teachers; however, teachers use a combination of traditional and progressive educational philosophies based on their personalities and teaching styles, and other factors that are discussed in Chapter 3. Teacher-centered, traditional philosophies rely on the teacher to be an expert on the content and to provide this information for students to learn. Teaching methods that are common in traditional classrooms are lecture, notetaking, testing, and memorization.

Student-centered, progressive philosophies expect the teacher to act as a facilitator or guide and students discover knowledge rather than passively receive it. Common teaching methods in progressive classrooms are discussion, question and answer, hands-on learning, and small groups. The student has the largest role in existentialism, because learning relies on the student to determine not only how to study but also what to study. A teacher will assist as needed, but what- or even if- the student learns is up to the student. Figure 1.3 shows how the student role in learning increases with the different educational philosophies.

Figure 1.3 Increasing Student Roles in Learning

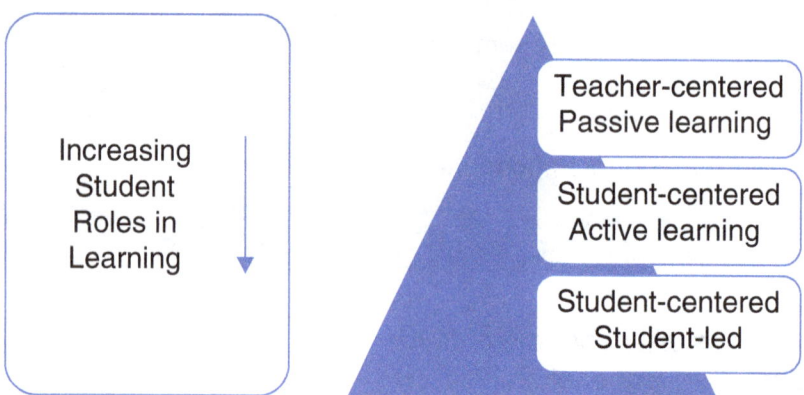

Source: April Graziano

Other Philosophical Considerations

The age/grade of students and the curriculum areas (art, math, science, etc.) play a part in why teachers teach the way they do. Many other factors also influence philosophical approaches to teaching and learning. As people study to become teachers, they learn about child development, psychology, and how people learn, and they observe and practice working in classrooms. When they become teachers, they are able to start teaching their own students in ways that they think will best help their students learn.

MEDIA EXTENSION FEATURE

Only a Teacher documentary series

Episode One

"A Teacher Affects Eternity"

http://www.pbs.org/onlyateacher/about1.html

Visit this PBS Webpage to read about Dean Eastman, a high school social studies teacher who is included in Episode One, discussing what he believes the teacher's role is and how he reaches out to students to help them stay in school. The educational philosophies of teachers at various times of American history are also presented throughout Episode One, and the video shows numerous photographs and journal entries from teachers in earlier times in our country.

STUDENT VOICES

"An idea that inspired me is learner autonomy. It's the idea that students take their own learning into their own hands. Students have control over how they gain information and use it to better their education. I think this is how education is supposed to be. Students should have the power to get an effective education by doing hands-on activities and challenge critical thinking skills."

Name _____   Date _____

Educational Philosophies

	Educational Philosophy	Characteristics	Positives & Negatives
Traditional	Essentialism	<ul><li></li><li></li><li></li><li></li><li></li><li></li><li></li></ul>	
	Perennialism	<ul><li></li><li></li><li></li><li></li><li></li><li></li><li></li></ul>	
Progressive	Progressivism	<ul><li></li><li></li><li></li><li></li><li></li><li></li><li></li></ul>	
	Social Reconstructionism	<ul><li></li><li></li><li></li><li></li><li></li><li></li><li></li></ul>	
	Existentialism	<ul><li></li><li></li><li></li><li></li><li></li><li></li><li></li></ul>	

Source: Adapted from Educational Philosophies worksheet

Field Experience Documentation Form 1

COLLEGE COURSE

College:
Course Number and Name:
Professor's Name:
Number of Required Hours:

COLLEGE STUDENT

Student's Name:
Student's College Email:
Student's Major:

OBSERVATION SITE

School or Center Name:
Address:

Phone Number:
Name of Principal or Director:
Name of Teacher(s) Observed:
Grade(s) or Subject Area(s) Observed:

OBSERVATIONS

Dates	Times	Number of Hours
	TOTAL HOURS	

SIGNATURES & DATES

Teacher(s) Observed:	
Student	
Professor:	

Field Experience Paper 1

Name _____ Due date _____

Total length required: Other requirements:

Respecting Confidentiality: Please be respectful of the teachers and children that you observe. Unless you have their permission, do not use their actual names in your papers. For teachers, you can abbreviate their names. For children, you can use a first name, but don't use a full name.

Answer the following questions in paper format without question numbers:

1. Where are you observing, and how many observation hours have you completed as of the date of this paper? (Write a paragraph of two or more sentences. Be sure to state the setting you are observing: public/private, school/afterschool/childcare, age/grade/subject.)
   For questions two to five, write a paragraph of three or more sentences to answer each question.
2. Describe the teaching and learning activities that you have observed. (What have the teachers and students done?)
3. What positive teacher characteristics have you observed, and how have those characteristics helped in the classroom?
4. What have you learned about teaching from observing in this setting? (teacher role, teaching methods, resources, learning styles, schedules, schools, issues, etc.)
5. Is this a teaching setting you would enjoy? Why or why not?

CHAPTER 2
Educational Organizations

> **STUDENT VOICES**
>
> "Initially I didn't really understand what a principal's job was, but I found that it seemed interesting after the discussion. While I personally think I would do better in a classroom setting, moving forward into being the principal seems like a good job if you can handle finance and people."

Vocabulary

Academic Organization
Associate's Degree
Bachelor's Degree
Charter
Doctorate
DOE
Higher Ed
Master's Degree
Primary School
School Committee
School District

Objectives

1. Communicate effectively with educational terms
2. Interpret data presented in graphs and charts about the field of education
3. Explore the nature and value of education in society
4. Demonstrate an understanding of education from historical, philosophical, social, and political frameworks
6. Develop knowledgeable, reflective, and critical perspectives of education
7. Debate current standards, requirements, and trends in early childhood through secondary education

Types of Schools

Parents are required by law to educate their children, and most parents enroll their children in their **school district**, which is the system of schools within a city, town, region, or other local area. Public schools are free to families who live in that district. Parents can choose to send their children to private schools instead, which are funded through tuition that families have to pay for their students to attend.

Schools are structured in a multitude of ways, and besides public and private schools, two other common types of education are charter schools and homeschooling. The exact parameters vary by state, but typically, charter schools are free to families. Charter schools are publicly funded, meaning they are paid for by state taxpayers. Unlike public schools, charter schools are established by an application to the state for permission

School district – A group of schools from a city, town, or region that share administrators and funding

(a **charter**) to open a school. New applications are reviewed annually and go through a selection process at the state level.

Approved charter schools are placed in public school districts by the state, and sometimes are opened even if the local public school district is opposed to having a charter school in its area. One reason a district might not want a charter school is because it might compete for the same students, taking students and funding away from the public schools. Another reason is that public school districts in some states are required to spend the district's funds for busing for charter school students even though charter schools receive their own funding.

Situations like this take funding from school districts that are typically already underfunded. However, for school districts that have a history of low success for students reaching grade-level skills and high failure rates, behavior issues, and dropout rates, charter schools can be a lifesaver for families who otherwise would have no options. Some charter schools are designed to follow a specific educational philosophy, and some offer challenging curriculum opportunities to help students explore their interests, become successful learners, and qualify for colleges.

Private schools also go through application and approval processes, but there are fewer new applications for private schools, and they are not publicly funded. They don't take many students and funds from school districts, so they usually aren't as controversial as charter schools sometimes are. Private schools can focus on special educational philosophies, curriculum areas, and/or include religious classes. The four basic types of schooling are outlined in Figure 2.1.

Charter– Permission from a state to begin a new school that is publicly funded but not in a school district, can be independent or part of a charter school network

Figure 2.1 Common Characteristics of Four Types of Schooling

Public Schools	Private Schools	Charter Schools	Homeschool
• No cost to families—cost to taxpayers	• Paid for by families—also pay taxes	• Public, but not—cost to taxpayers	• Paid for by families
• Curriculum—state requirements	• Some state requirements	• State requirements and charter req.	• District approval of curriculum plan
• Must educate <u>all</u> children by law	• Application—limited seats	• Application—limited seats, waiting list	• District approval—who participates
• School choice—apply to attend other district	• Sometimes include homeschool students for special courses	• Sometimes participate in public school support services	• Sometimes partic. in coop w/ other families
• If large district—lots of course choices	• Limited courses unless elite school	• Can have special academic focus	• Sometimes partic. in public or private lab/gym or other course

Source: April Graziano

School Grade Levels

Schools are often described by the ages and grade levels they have, such as elementary (kindergarten through 6th grade), middle (grades 5–6), junior high (grades 7–8), and high schools (grades 9–12). Many school districts are now offering part- or full-time preschool programs in their elementary buildings to help children learn and get ready for kindergarten.

Middle and junior high schools can be combined into one, or grades 7 to 8 could be included in a junior and senior high school. There are many other combinations that have different grades. **Primary schools** have one or more lower elementary grades such as only kindergarten or PK-2, and K-8 schools have kindergarten to 8th-grade students.

Preschools can be public or private childcare centers, can be located in schools or community centers, or they can be in home childcare centers. Preschool has proven to be very beneficial for young children, helping them prepare for kindergarten. Children can also be prepared if their parents read to them, talk with them, and involve them in learning about their daily environments (home, library, family, church, playground, grocery store, etc.). But many of today's children are not prepared because their families don't know how to help them learn, family members have to work several jobs, and there sometimes aren't enough quality childcare programs available for everyone. One possible solution to this is universal preschool, providing free preschool to every child. There are many positives and negatives to this idea, and there would need to be many more qualified preschool teachers to meet this need if funding were provided for universal preschool.

School Funding

How schools are paid for is called **school funding**, which includes employees, buildings, furniture, utilities, resources for students and teachers, field trips, special events, and so on. Public schools are free for students to attend, but they are paid for by state and local taxes, funds from the federal government, grant funding, and fundraisers. Each state's budget includes funding for education in the state: preschool-grade 12 schools, colleges, charter schools, and special programs and initiatives. The amounts vary greatly from one state or school district to another, but every public school district gets some state funding and some local funding. Charter schools also get school funding from state taxes, but private schools do not.

State support for education is determined by the state legislators (senators and representatives who work in the state capitol). When citizens want to increase the amount of school funding, they can contact their legislators, and they can ask for a question about a tax increase to be added to the voting ballots. Property taxes in a city or town also contribute to school funding, and voters can approve a ballot question about raising funds for schools where they live.

School Administration

Principals lead schools and supervise teachers, but there are many levels of administrators over the principals as shown in Figure 2.2. The principal reports to the school district superintendent, and the superintendent reports to the **school committee** (or school board), which is legally responsible for helping to lead the school district. In most districts, school committee members are volunteers who run for election to serve on the committee.

The state department of education (**DOE**) oversees all of the school districts in that state, regardless of whether the schools are public, private, or charter schools. The state DOE answers to the governor, who works with the state legislators to lead education efforts and approve education funding. In some states like Massachusetts, there is another level between the state DOE and the governor, a secretary

Figure 2.2 School Administration

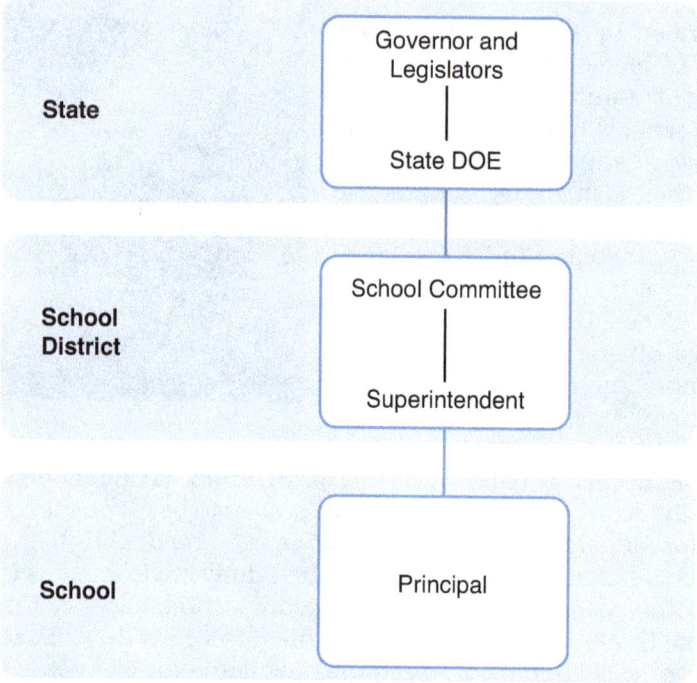

Source: April Graziano

of education who is appointed by the governor to oversee the state DOE.

Federal Government

There is a federal DOE that helps support education in America. However, except for federal laws, most educational decisions are made at the state level. The federal government works with the US senators and representatives to create and revise educational laws, and they work with the president to provide several different types of funding for educational efforts. Some federal funding goes directly to the state DOEs, while other funding is offered through grant applications for specific programs.

MEDIA EXTENSION FEATURE

Waiting for Superman

Failing public schools, turnaround efforts, teachers' unions, and charter schools are a few of the topics presented in the documentary, **Waiting for Superman**. This is a very visual way to explore difficult topics in education, and there are many web resources about it, including an online discussion on the **Public School Review** website about the issues in the film and details about the positive and negative responses to it: https://www.publicschoolreview.com/blog/waiting-for-superman-the-heroes-and-the-villains-of-education.

Other Educational Organizations

Higher Ed (higher education) refers to colleges and universities. Someone who graduates from high school earns a diploma. In higher ed, people earn college degrees based on amount and level of the courses they take. People can earn an **Associate's degree**, which is about two years of full-time college (at least 60 credits completed). A **Bachelor's degree** is equivalent to about four years of full-time college (at least 120 credits completed). Some students earn an Associate's degree and then transfer into a Bachelor's degree program. Other students enter a Bachelor's degree program directly. Both of these approaches have benefits for future teachers, and all states require teachers to earn at least a Bachelor's degree in education.

After earning a Bachelor's degree, the next degree level is a **Master's degree**, and teacher salary levels are higher for teachers who earn this degree. In three states, Massachusetts, New York, and Ohio, teachers can start teaching with a Bachelor's degree, but they must earn a Master's degree within five years. Finally, the degree after a Master's is a **Doctorate**, and it is the highest college degree level. Figure 2.3 shows the levels of college degrees.

College degrees build on each other, but it's also possible to have different degrees in related areas. For example, a future teacher could get an Associate's degree in Elementary Education and then get a Bachelor's degree in Elementary Education. That person could start teaching with the Bachelor's degree earning a full-time salary and benefits, and then earn a Master's degree in Reading and a Doctorate in Curriculum. More information about teacher training is given in Chapter 4 and Chapter 6.

Figure 2.3 Degrees in Higher Education

Source: April Graziano

A teachers' union or **teachers' association** is a union for teachers in a school district, state, region, and/or country. Like other unions, a teachers' union provides benefits for teachers and helps promote changes to improve teaching and learning. The union is often named by the school district or state, such as the Springfield Teachers' Union, the Massachusetts Teachers' Association (MTA), or the National Education Association (NEA). Teachers' unions help protect teachers' rights and help negotiate teacher contracts for school districts.

Parents can join together to help their children's schools. A parent group is called the Parent Teacher Organization (**PTO**) or the Parent Teacher Association (**PTA**). A school's PTO will help lead school fundraisers, participate in school events, and help parents and teachers communication with each other.

Academic organizations provide teachers with current information about academic areas, help them learn from other educators, and help provide professional development for teachers. Some examples of organizations are shown in Figure 2.4.

Figure 2.4 Examples of Academic Organizations for Educators

NCTM—National Council of Teachers of Mathematics	NCTE—National Council of Teachers of English	ISTE—International Society for Technology in Education
NCSS—National Council for Social Studies	AASL—American Association of School Librarians	NSTA—National Science Teachers Association

Source: April Graziano

STUDENT VOICES

"This interview really showed how different each district and each school is. It portrayed how a job at one school could have more or less responsibilities at another."

Name _____ Date _____

Venn Diagram

SAMPLE Characteristics of Two School Districts

Name of School District A _____

Name of School District B _____

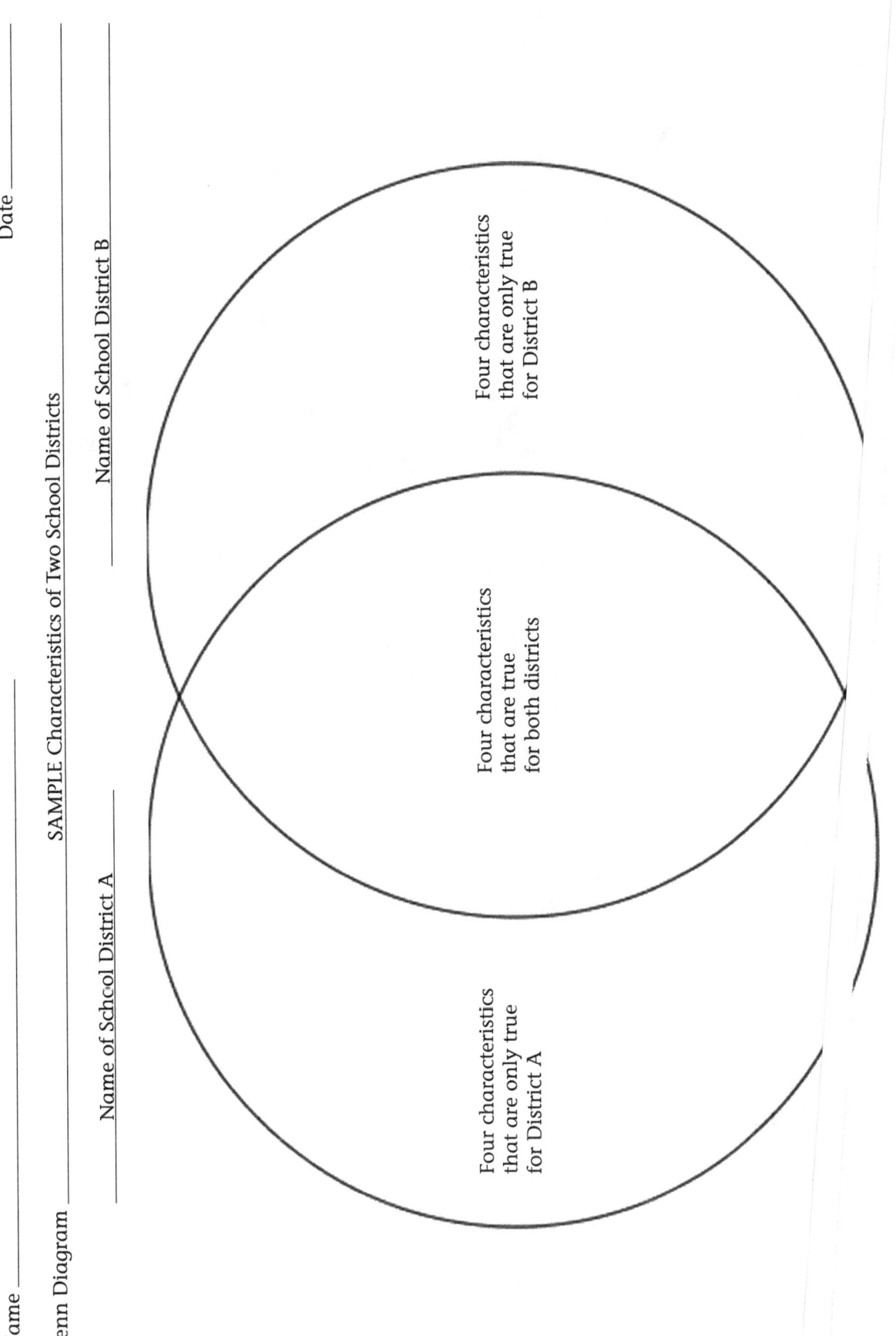

Four characteristics that are only true for District A

Four characteristics that are true for both districts

Four characteristics that are only true for District B

Student Learning Outcomes: Explore the nature and value of education in society
Develop knowledgeable, reflective, and critical perspectives of education

Name _____

Due date _____

Venn Diagram _____

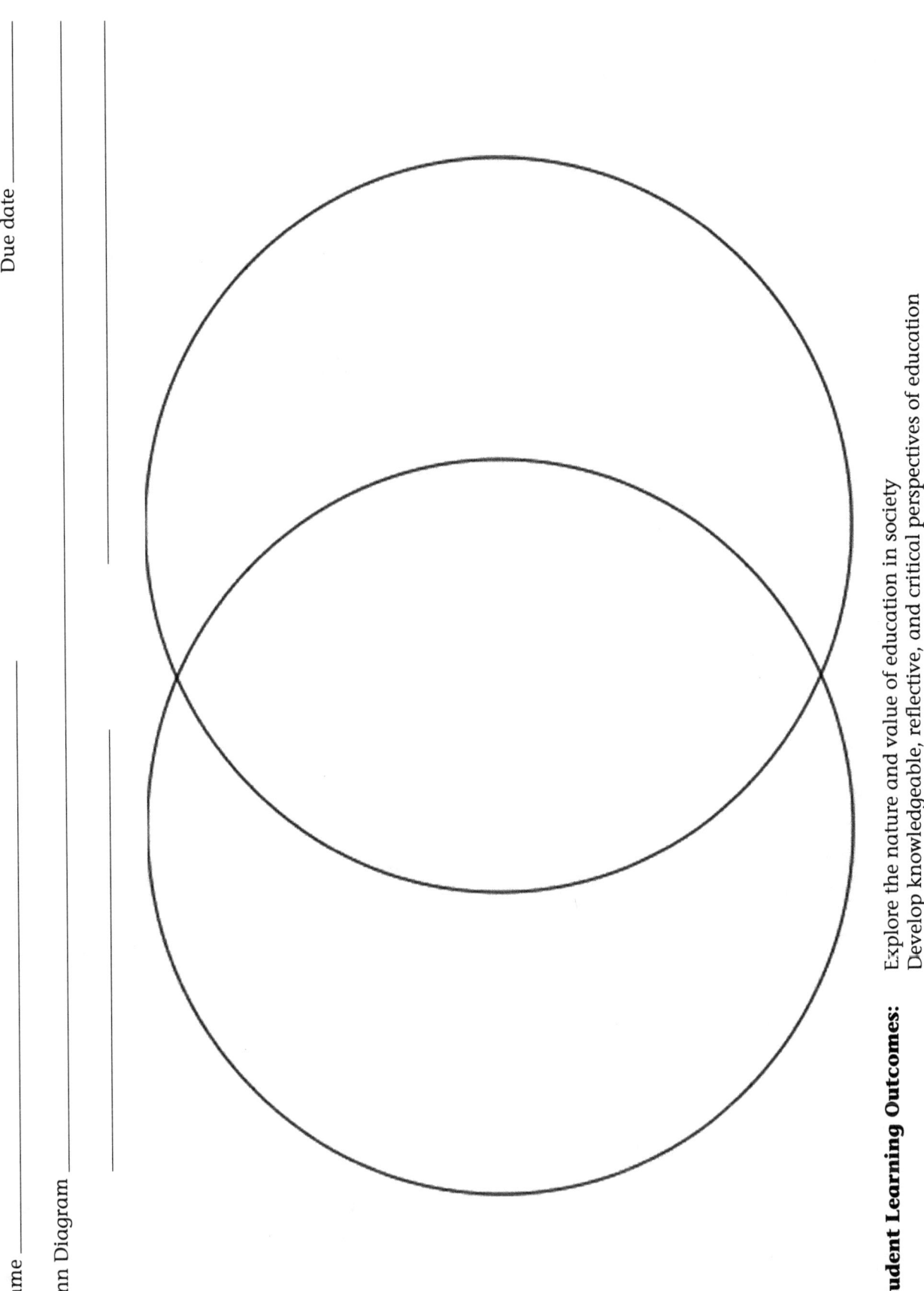

Student Learning Outcomes: Explore the nature and value of education in society
Develop knowledgeable, reflective, and critical perspectives of education

Chapter 2: Educational Organizations 27

Table 235.20 Revenues for public elementary and secondary schools, by source of funds and state or jurisdiction: 2016-17

[In current dollars]

State or jurisdiction	Total (in thousands)	Federal			State		Local (including intermediate sources below the state level)			Property taxes		Private\2\	
		Amount (in thousands)	Per pupil	Percent of total	Amount (in thousands)	Percent of total	Amount (in thousands)\1\	Percent of total		Amount (in thousands)	Percent of total	Amount (in thousands)	Percent of total
1	2	3	4	5	6	7	8	9		10	11	12	13
United States			$1,135	8.1		47.0		44.9			36.6		1.7
Alabama	7,889,120	863,637	1,159	10.9	4,350,890	55.2	2,674,593	33.9		1,223,602	15.5	325,777	4.1
Alaska	2,508,281	354,045	2,667	14.1	1,600,510	63.8	553,726	22.1		319,889	12.8	18,951	0.8
Arizona	10,259,496	1,326,469	1,191	12.9	4,778,454	46.6	4,154,572	40.5		3,182,393	31.0	248,513	2.4
Arkansas	5,619,332	625,993	1,269	11.1	2,950,895	52.5	2,042,443	36.3		1,782,061	31.7	158,048	2.8
California	88,108,864	7,455,046	1,182	8.5	50,841,072	57.7	29,812,746	33.8		24,101,208	27.4	394,460	0.4
Colorado	10,600,561	706,162	780	6.7	4,602,299	43.4	5,292,101	49.9		4,287,369	40.4	393,355	3.7
Connecticut	11,583,918	503,812	941	4.3	4,494,453	38.8	6,585,653	56.9		6,431,528	55.5	92,242	0.8
Delaware	2,729,986	188,717	1,385	6.9	1,323,678	48.5	1,217,591	44.6		646,622	23.7	17,771	0.7
District of Columbia	2,526,099	237,820	2,770	9.4	†	†	2,288,279	90.6		767,117	30.4	11,358	0.4
Florida	28,808,723	3,288,570	1,167	11.4	11,346,675	39.4	14,173,479	49.2		11,738,747	40.7	935,775	3.2
Georgia	2,04,43,717	19,25,205	1,091	9.4	94,39,804	46.2	90,78,707	44.4		60,20,224	29.4	4,74,428	2.3
Hawaii	28,44,167	2,52,145	1,389	8.9	25,34,177	89.1	57,844	2.0		0	0.0	28,852	1.0
Idaho	25,75,178	2,52,533	850	9.8	17,06,894	66.3	6,15,751	23.9		5,17,769	20.1	35,395	1.4
Illinois	3,54,80,443	23,12,325	1,141	6.5	1,37,10,764	38.6	1,94,57,354	54.8		1,70,82,907	48.1	4,80,875	1.4
Indiana	1,19,52,546	9,74,150	928	8.2	70,87,311	59.3	38,91,085	32.6		30,05,433	25.1	3,42,023	2.9
Iowa	69,04,458	4,97,385	976	7.2	37,32,324	54.1	26,74,750	38.7		21,87,985	31.7	1,45,240	2.1
Kansas	63,44,151	5,37,797	1,088	8.5	40,31,070	63.5	17,75,284	28.0		11,03,725	17.4	1,52,835	2.4
Kentucky	77,82,860	9,12,224	1,334	11.7	42,29,780	54.3	26,40,856	33.9		19,75,137	25.4	85,541	1.1
Louisiana	89,49,726	11,68,690	1,632	13.1	39,03,101	43.6	38,77,936	43.3		16,89,558	18.9	50,474	0.6
Maine	28,20,246	1,95,168	1,081	6.9	10,93,382	38.8	15,31,696	54.3		14,57,658	51.7	36,636	1.3
Maryland	1,50,45,717	8,51,860	961	5.7	66,25,703	44.0	75,68,154	50.3		37,03,439	24.6	1,15,109	0.8

(Continued)

Table 235.20 Revenues for public elementary and secondary schools, by source of funds and state or jurisdiction: 2016-17 (Continued)

[In current dollars]

State or jurisdiction	Total (in thousands)	Federal			State		Local (including intermediate sources below the state level)		Property taxes		Private\2\	
		Amount (in thousands)	Per pupil	Percent of total	Amount (in thousands)	Percent of total	Amount (in thousands)\1\	Percent of total	Amount (in thousands)	Percent of total	Amount (in thousands)	Percent of total
Massachusetts	1,84,23,533	9,29,798	964	5.0	69,99,777	38.0	1,04,93,958	57.0	97,66,156	53.0	2,73,640	1.5
Michigan	2,01,63,387	17,34,557	1,135	8.6	1,22,24,090	60.6	62,04,741	30.8	52,89,166	26.2	2,73,047	1.4
Minnesota	1,32,42,082	7,43,953	850	5.6	87,62,296	66.2	37,35,833	28.2	24,49,514	18.5	3,50,318	2.6
Mississippi	47,53,225	6,72,881	1,393	14.2	24,15,769	50.8	16,64,576	35.0	13,93,467	29.3	1,10,153	2.3
Missouri	1,14,85,402	10,03,289	1,096	8.7	37,49,129	32.6	67,32,984	58.6	52,86,304	46.0	3,49,579	3.0
Montana	18,41,286	2,25,892	1,543	12.3	8,67,286	47.1	7,48,107	40.6	4,76,318	25.9	62,801	3.4
Nebraska	44,70,153	3,49,144	1,094	7.8	14,50,774	32.5	26,70,235	59.7	23,69,879	53.0	1,61,587	3.6
Nevada	49,19,401	4,44,730	939	9.0	17,80,380	36.2	26,94,292	54.8	12,01,302	24.4	28,596	0.6
New Hampshire	31,32,306	1,73,816	961	5.5	10,07,310	32.2	19,51,180	62.3	18,59,886	59.4	46,040	1.5
New Jersey	30,368,383	1,269,661	900	4.2	12,920,845	42.5	16,177,878	53.3	15,304,628	50.4	581,364	1.9
New Mexico	4,023,795	589,017	1,752	14.6	2,726,305	67.8	708,473	17.6	572,792	14.2	54,087	1.3
New York	69,228,226	3,657,578	1,373	5.3	28,253,045	40.8	37,317,603	53.9	34,657,273	50.1	305,467	0.4
North Carolina	14,481,275	1,641,260	1,059	11.3	9,057,842	62.5	3,782,173	26.1	3,290,986	22.7	166,817	1.2
North Dakota	1,757,100	163,446	1,490	9.3	1,014,779	57.8	578,875	32.9	423,505	24.1	69,564	4.0
Ohio	24,762,785	1,949,822	1,140	7.9	10,538,278	42.6	12,274,685	49.6	10,070,121	40.7	642,876	2.6
Oklahoma	6,361,194	726,159	1,046	11.4	3,007,742	47.3	2,627,292	41.3	2,007,824	31.6	281,400	4.4
Oregon	7,689,411	550,627	951	7.2	4,018,900	52.3	3,119,884	40.6	2,524,905	32.8	137,680	1.8
Pennsylvania	31,353,132	2,152,130	1,246	6.9	12,104,094	38.6	17,096,908	54.5	13,601,256	43.4	385,862	1.2
Rhode Island	2,561,477	192,929	1,357	7.5	1,087,361	42.5	1,281,187	50.0	1,242,366	48.5	25,406	1.0
South Carolina	9,992,973	913,225	1,184	9.1	4,867,687	48.7	4,212,060	42.2	3,195,782	32.0	245,374	2.5

(Continued)

Table 235.20 Revenues for public elementary and secondary schools, by source of funds and state or jurisdiction: 2016-17 *(Continued)*

[In current dollars]

State or jurisdiction	Total (in thousands)	Federal			State		Local (including intermediate sources below the state level)		Property taxes		Private\2\	
		Amount (in thousands)	Per pupil	Percent of total	Amount (in thousands)	Percent of total	Amount (in thousands)\1\	Percent of total	Amount (in thousands)	Percent of total	Amount (in thousands)	Percent of total
South Dakota	1,580,004	205,299	1,506	13.0	540,408	34.2	834,297	52.8	716,885	45.4	44,816	2.8
Tennessee	10,077,253	1,161,635	1,160	11.5	4,629,304	45.9	4,286,312	42.5	2,008,470	19.9	438,170	4.3
Texas	60,005,975	6,298,581	1,175	10.5	23,339,969	38.9	30,368,425	50.6	27,675,817	46.1	1,022,545	1.7
Utah	5,757,609	459,308	696	8.0	3,183,265	55.3	2,115,036	36.7	1,598,326	27.8	241,408	4.2
Vermont	17,42,206	1,13,773	1,287	6.5	15,60,743	89.6	67,685	3.9	2,385	0.1	21,859	1.3
Virginia	1,66,11,639	11,31,683	879	6.8	65,65,661	39.5	89,14,296	53.7	53,99,824	32.5	2,41,647	1.5
Washington	1,56,54,623	10,71,035	972	6.8	98,46,364	62.9	47,37,224	30.3	40,56,493	25.9	2,99,337	1.9
West Virginia	35,26,416	4,04,295	1,476	11.5	19,17,056	54.4	12,05,066	34.2	11,15,409	31.6	19,618	0.6
Wisconsin	1,15,91,278	8,32,985	964	7.2	53,60,746	46.2	53,97,548	46.6	48,91,353	42.2	2,24,031	1.9
Wyoming	19,31,277	1,18,429	1,258	6.1	11,41,567	59.1	6,71,281	34.8	4,86,856	25.2	16,436	0.9
Other jurisdictions												
American Samoa	73,876	62,905	—	85.2	10,738	14.5	232	0.3	0	0.0	14	#
Guam	332,552	60,166	1,956	18.1	0	0.0	272,386	81.9	0	0.0	147	#
Northern Marianas	87,683	39,503	—	45.1	47,227	53.9	953	1.1	0	0.0	711	0.8
Puerto Rico	2,819,791	935,887	2,563	33.2	1,883,850	66.8	55	#	0	0.0	55	#
U.S. Virgin Islands	193,314	26,259	1,990	13.6	0	0.0	167,056	86.4	0	0.0	5	#

—Not available.
†Not applicable.
#Rounds to zero.
\1\Includes other categories of revenue not separately shown.
\2\Includes revenues from gifts, and tuition and fees from patrons.

Note: Excludes revenues for state education agencies. Detail may not sum to totals because of rounding.

Source: U.S. Department of Education, National Center for Education Statistics, Common Core of Data (CCD), "National Public Education Financial Survey," 2016-17. (This table was prepared August 2019.)

Section I—School Funding in the News

Name _____ Due date _____

Required length:

Other requirements:

Directions:

1. Search online to find a news article about school funding in your area or another part of the country. Be sure to select an article from a reputable source. Then answer the following questions:
   Name of article:
   Author(s):
   Publication date:
   Source (Website name, title of news broadcast, URL, or other identifying information):

2. What school funding problem or situation is discussed in the article?

3. What do you think the author's bias is about the article? Why do you think that?

4. Is a resolution to the funding situation discussed in the article? If so, state what solution is mentioned. If not, tell what you think should be done.

5. Do you disagree or agree with his article or someone mentioned in the article? Why?

6. What other questions or ideas did the article make you think of?

Chapter 2: Educational Organizations   33

Name _____   Due date _____

Section I – Issues and Trends in Education

Directions

1) Consider the educational issues and trends that were discussed in Section I The Field of Education. Think about the arguments related to each issue, and then show how much you disagree or agree by placing that issue on the following line:

   Charter Schools—Every state should help establish more charter schools.
   Educational Funding—The current level of funding is sufficient for the needs of students.
   Failing Schools—All American schools are successful in some ways.
   Mandated Schooling—Students should be required to attend school until 18 years old.
   Student-Centered Teaching—All student-centered philosophies will lead to increased learning.
   Turnaround Plans—A school or district that is failing can be turned around to succeed.
   Universal Preschool—Every child should be required to attend preschool.

2) Place a dot on the diagram for each item and label the items.

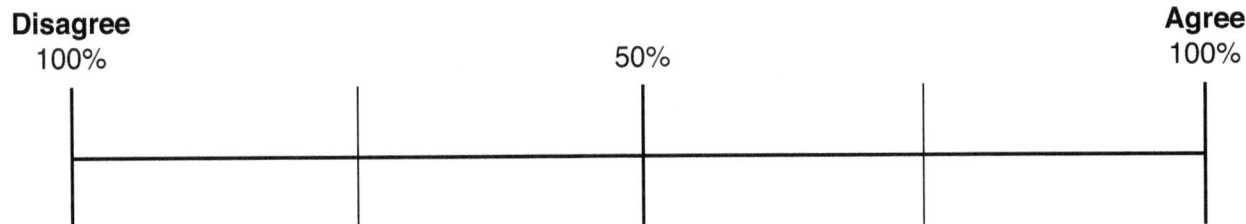

3) For each issue, explain why you put the item where you did. What parts of the topics or statements do you disagree or agree with?

   Charter Schools—Every state should help establish more charter schools.

   Educational Funding—The current level of funding is sufficient for the needs of students.

Failing Schools—All American schools are successful in some ways.

Mandated Schooling—Students should be required to attend school until 18 years old.

Student-Centered Teaching—All student-centered philosophies will lead to increased learning.

Turnaround Plans—A school or district that is failing can be turned around to succeed.

Universal Preschool—Every child should be required to attend preschool.

SECTION II
Quality Educators

> **STUDENT VOICES**
>
> "Education changes all the time, just like any profession. If new regulations and guidelines emerge, I think classes should be offered to get the school on board with new, upcoming topics. Also, sometimes teachers need to understand the new generation to really capture what they need to know about their class and students."

Chapters

3 Art and Science   37
4 Highly Qualified   47
5 Teacher and Student Diversity   63
6 Benefits and Challenges of Teaching   95

Current Issues and Trends to Be Explored

Arming Teachers
Class Size
No-Zero Grading Policy
School Violence
Teacher Preparation
Teacher Diversity
Teacher Salary

CHAPTER 3
Art and Science

STUDENT VOICES

"To be a successful teacher, a person needs to be kind and understanding of the different circumstances kids come into the classroom with. Teachers need to be trained to cater to that and be flexible enough to adjust how they teach to fit the students' needs. They also need to bring in topics that students are interested in to keep them engaged, focused, and on task without them getting bored and not actively learning."

Vocabulary

Class Size
Pedagogy
Pedagogical
Policy
Rubric
Student to Teacher Ratio

© Romariolen/Shutterstock.com

Objectives

1. Communicate effectively with educational terms
2. Interpret data presented in graphs and charts about the field of education
4. Demonstrate an understanding of education from historical, philosophical, social, and political frameworks
5. Explore the role of schools in maintaining, perpetuating, and influencing culture, both nationally and internationally
6. Develop knowledgeable, reflective, and critical perspectives of education
7. Debate current standards, requirements, and trends in early childhood through secondary education

The Art and Science of Teaching

Teaching is sometimes described as being part art and part science. **Pedagogy**, sometimes known as the art and science of teaching, is a term for all the things that teachers know and do. It isn't a label for the grades or subject areas they teach, but it is a combination of teacher creativity, teacher training and coursework, and teacher experience.

Pedagogy– Ped/a/go/gy— How and why teachers teach; their skills and creativity

The Art of Teaching

Teachers' personalities play a big role in engaging their students and developing trust. Teaching involves a lot of creativity. Finding topics and approaches that will help their students enjoy learning, finding new ways to communicate with students, using artistic talent to decorate a classroom, or using funny voices for story characters are just a few of the ways that teachers get to be creative.

In addition to creativity, aspects of the art of teaching are choosing just the right teaching method or idea for students, ways of responding to students, ways to motivate students, and problem solving throughout the school day.

The Science of Teaching

Teachers' educational philosophy, experience, and content knowledge are part of the science of teaching. Other aspects include knowledge of how people learn, how to measure student learning, and child development. Current research about **pedagogical** approaches helps teachers continue to build the skills and knowledge they need to be effective teachers. Examples of teacher characteristics are given in Figure 3.1.

Pedagogical– Ped/a/gog/i/cal—Related to teaching E.g., a pedagogical method

Class Size

The number of students assigned to a class is called **class size**. The number of students compared to the number of teachers is called the **student to teacher ratio**. If there are 23 students and one teacher in a class, the student to teacher ratio is 23:1. In education, class size discussions are usually talking about whether or not the number of students

Figure 3.1 Examples of Teaching Skills

Art of Teaching
- Creativity
- Character traits
- Personality
- Teaching methods
- Brainstorming
- Responding to students
- Measuring student learning
- Problem solving
- Flexibility

Science of Teaching
- Educational philosophy
- Content knowledge (subject area knowledge
- Assessment
- Grading
- Child development
- Educational research
- Time management
- Issues and trends in education

Source: April Graziano

in a class has an impact on how well those students learn. Most people would agree that having fewer students in a class would mean that the teacher would be able to spend more time with each student. When class sizes are smaller, it is more expensive for a school district because it has to hire more teachers.

Another way that class size impacts teaching is how a teacher manages a classroom, the types of teaching methods that will work with the number of students in a given class space, and the pedagogical approaches that feel comfortable in that classroom. There needs to be enough space for the students to safely move throughout the room and for the teaching and learning resources to be used. Figure 3.2 shows that the average class size in public schools in 2017 to 2018 ranged from 16 to 26, depending on the type of class and school.

MEDIA EXTENSION FEATURE

Numerous Hollywood movies have been made to show how an amazing teacher who doesn't give up on students can change students' lives. Keep in mind that the movies listed below are fictionalized accounts. They are not factual biographies, but they are inspirational.

Jaime Escalante

Stand and Deliver

Erin Gruwell

The Freedom Writers

Figure 3.2 Average Public School Class Size, 2017 to 2018

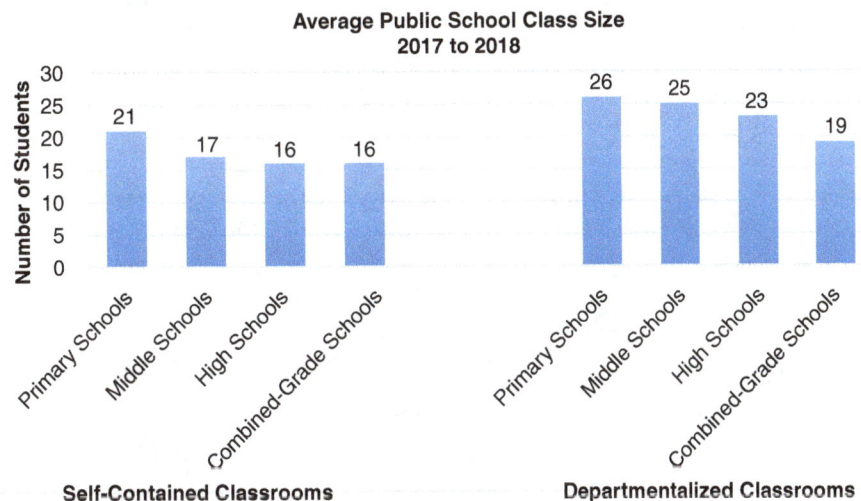

Source: Characteristics of Public and Private Elementary and Secondary School Teachers in the United States: Results from the 2017 to 18 National Teacher and Principal Survey

Grading

Giving students grades for their work can involve a wide variety of skills, because teachers use their educational philosophy, reasoning, and sometimes a sense of the degree of the correctness of student work. Teachers also use mathematical reasoning, knowledge of assessment, and knowledge of grading methods to determine what grade to assign. Sometimes teachers use **rubrics**, tables that list the detailed expectations for an assignment and help determine the value of each part of an assignment, grading each area on a number scale such as one to four, with four being the highest points for a part of the assignment such as using transitions in writing.

School district policies determine what a letter grade is worth and which letter grades are used. For example, in one district an A is equal to 93% to 96%. In other district, an A is equal to 93% to 100% because they don't use A+. A **policy** is a rule or procedure determined by a governing agency. School policies are determined by principals, superintendents, school committees, and the state department of education (DOE), and teachers have to follow them.

Policy– A decision made by a governing authority about how something will be done

---

MEDIA EXTENSION FEATURE

Should there be a no-zero grading policy?

YES—There IS a no-zero grading policy. Zeros aren't allowed.

"How to Create a No-Zero Policy in Your Classroom" by TeachThought Staff, 1/30/19

https://www.teachthought.com/pedagogy/installing-a-no-zero-policy/

NO—There ISN'T a no-zero grading policy. Teachers can give zeros.

"Why I Still Give My Students Zeros" by Ray Salazar, 4/4/19

https://www.nbpts.org/why-i-still-give-my-students-zeros/

No-Zero Grading Policy

Teachers have a lot of choices in the way they teach and run their classes, but they must make sure that what they do follows the policies that govern their work.

A no-zero grading policy means that teachers are not allowed to give zeroes as grades. Everyone can relate to issues about grading; however, this topic can be confusing because a no-zero grading policy means that school districts decide to not let teachers give students grades of zero. The argument is about *whether or not there should be a policy* about this. So, YES means that <u>zeros aren't allowed</u>, and NO means that there isn't a policy restricting teachers' grading and they <u>can give zeros</u>.

STUDENT VOICES
"It is important to students to be engaged in their reading . . . I always struggled getting through a class book, literally fighting to stay focused and keep my eyes open, but if the reading was something of my interest it made a world of a difference."

Memorable Teacher

Name _____ Due date _____

Required length:

Other requirements:

Directions:
Think about the most memorable teacher that you've ever had or that you've known. What elements of the art and science of teaching did that teacher demonstrate? Do you have any characteristics in common with that teacher, or do you have different types of personalities? What impact did that teacher have on your life?

_____
_____
_____
_____
_____
_____
_____
_____
_____
_____
_____
_____
_____
_____
_____
_____
_____
_____
_____
_____

Chapter 3: Art and Science 45

Reflective Writing

Name _____ Due date _____

Required length:

Other requirements:

Directions:

1. Select one of the photographs from Chapter 3 to write about aspects of the art and science of teaching. Which picture did you choose? Circle the letter of your answer.

   A. Geography teacher
   B. Teacher at table with toddlers
   C. High school teacher and students in a library
   D. Students working in a group around a table
   E. Middle school teacher and students in front of a whiteboard

2. Brainstorm at least 10 words or phrases that you think of when you see the photo.

3. Describe how the image is related to the art and/or the science of teaching. You can use one of the following questions or use another approach in your writing, and you can use the back of this page if you need more room.

   A. What do you like or dislike about the photo? Why?
   B. Would you change this photo in any way? Why?

CHAPTER 4
Highly Qualified

STUDENT VOICES

"While thinking about educational philosophy, teacher training, and teacher licensing, I feel there are plenty of things to come into play. It is a privilege to become an educator. I feel all educators should perform at their highest level of teaching to make every student succeed."

Vocabulary

Certification
Highly Qualified
License
Licensure
No Child Left Behind Act (NCLB)
Practicum
Reciprocity
Teacher Candidate
Teacher Preparation

Objectives

1. Communicate effectively with educational terms
2. Interpret data presented in graphs and charts about the field of education
6. Develop knowledgeable, reflective, and critical perspectives of education
7. Debate current standards, requirements, and trends in early childhood through secondary education
8. Identify the degree to which one's strengths and interests are consistent with the demands of teaching and related professions

Highly Qualified Teachers

In discussing how well trained a teacher is, if a teacher is fully trained according to state regulations for the grade or subject area the teacher is teaching, then that teacher is considered **highly qualified**. This phrase comes from the No Child Left Behind Act (**NCLB**), and helps school districts distinguish between those teachers who are fully qualified and any teachers who are teaching in an area they were not trained for, or who are still completing advanced degrees that are required by the state. A Master's degree is an advanced degree that is often required for teachers. Not all states require teachers to have a Master's degree to teach in public schools, while others require all teachers of all grades (preschool to 12th grade) to have a Master's. Whatever the requirements are, a teacher who has met all requirements is highly qualified.

Highly qualified–Having met all requirements for the grade or subject area being taught

NCLB–No Child Left Behind Act, the common name for a reauthorization of the federal government's Elementary and Secondary Education Act

Teacher Characteristics

According to a national survey of teachers and principals in 2017 to 2018, 79% of American teachers in public schools were white, 7% were black, and 9% were Hispanic. In private schools, 85% of teachers were white, 3% were black, and 7% were Hispanic (Characteristics, 3). This data is shown in Figure 4.1, and diversity is further discussed in Chapter 5.

Figure 4.1 Racial/Ethnic Backgrounds of Public and Private School Teachers

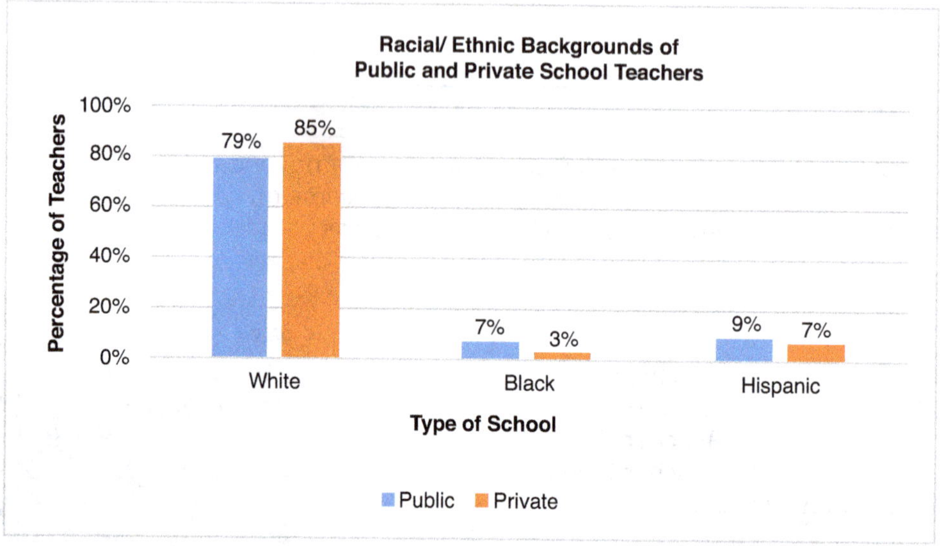

Source: Characteristics of Public and Private Elementary and Secondary School Teachers in the United States: Results from the 2017 to 2018 National Teacher and Principal Survey, April 2020

MEDIA EXTENSION FEATURE

The Value of Teacher Leadership

https://www.youtube.com/watch?v=tMLIZHeOlEk&feature=youtu.be

Teachers can be valuable leaders in their districts. By helping teachers become leaders, districts can help keep those teacher leaders working within their schools.

Teachers in charter schools had an average of 10 years of experience in teaching, and public and private school teachers had an average of 14 years of experience. Charter school teachers were an average of 39 years old, public school teachers were an average of 43 years old, and private school teachers were an average of 44 years old (Characteristics, 3).

Teacher Preparation Programs

The teacher preparation requirements can be the same for all types of educators, or the requirements can be different for special positions or school types. All states require at least a Bachelor's degree for classroom and specialist teachers such as art, music, physical education, and technology, regardless of the age level of the students. However, three states allow teachers to start teaching with a Bachelor's but require a Master's degree within five years: Massachusetts, New York, and Ohio. In Massachusetts, the degree requirement is the same for all public school teachers, from preschool to 12th grade.

Generally, a position that requires a deeper level of knowledge about curriculum and assessment and plays a leadership role in a school will have a higher degree requirement. Examples of teaching positions that usually require Master's degrees are principals, reading resource teachers, library teachers, and curriculum directors. Many principals and most superintendents have Doctorate degrees, a level after Masters. The degrees held by teachers in public and private schools in 2017-2018 are shown in Figure 4.2.

Figure 4.2 Highest Academic Degrees Held by Public and Private School Teachers, 2017 to 2018

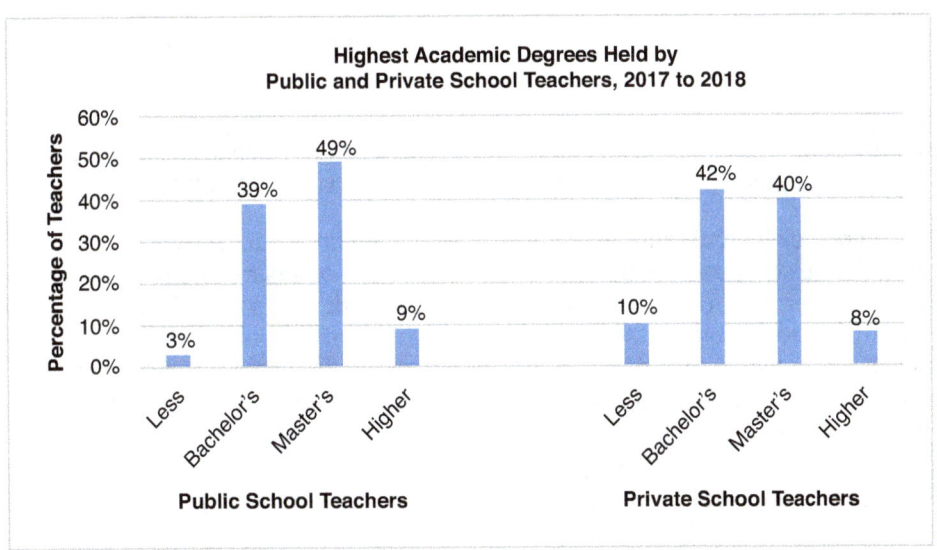

Source: Characteristics of Public and Private Elementary and Secondary School Teachers in the United States: Results from the 2017 to 2018 National Teacher and Principal Survey, April 2020

Coursework

College courses in teacher preparation programs vary by state and by college. Most but not all public school teachers had coursework in lesson planning, learning assessment, and classroom management. Figure 4.3 shows that fewer private school teachers had coursework in these and in all areas than teachers in public schools. The skill areas that 70% or fewer public school teachers and less than 50% of private school teachers studied were in serving students with special needs, serving students from diverse economic backgrounds, using student performance data to inform instruction, and teaching students who are limited-English proficient or English language learners.

Teacher candidates are college students who are completing degrees to become teachers. To be well prepared to teach starting on day one, all teacher candidates should have coursework in all of these areas and in the content areas they will teach. Not training new teachers to skillfully plan and assess learning or to support learning for all students does not give them the tools they need to be effective, greatly reducing the quality of education that their students receive.

Teacher candidate— Someone who is in college to become a teacher

Figure 4.3 Graduate or Undergraduate Coursework Prior to First Year of Teaching

Gratuate of Undergradute Coursework Prior to First Year of Teaching

[Bar chart showing Public vs Private percentages for: Lesson planning, Learning assessment, Classroom management techniques, Serving students with special needs, Serving students from diverse economic..., Using student performance data to inform..., Teaching students who are limited-English...]

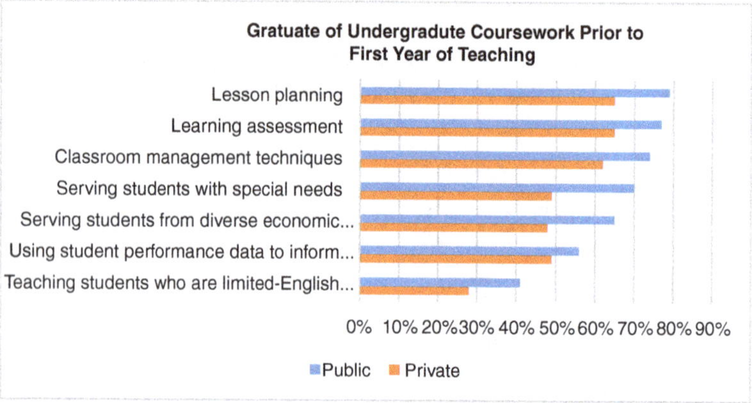

Source: Characteristics of Public and Private Elementary and Secondary School Teachers in the United States: Results from the 2017 to 2018 National Teacher and Principal Survey, April 2020

In most states, there are different training requirements for preschool teachers who teach in childcare centers instead of schools. Some states require an Associate's degree and others require a Bachelor's degree for lead teachers. Assistant teachers are not required to complete coursework. Teachers who are in preschool classrooms in public schools in Massachusetts must meet all the requirements of public school teachers for all grades: Bachelor's degree to begin teaching, then a Master's degree within five years. Teacher candidates for preschool to 12th grade must also complete practicum courses, also called student teaching, when they practice teaching in classroom with mentor teachers and students. Qualifications by state are listed in Figure 4.4.

Figure 4.4 State Preschool Standards and Teacher Qualifications, 2016 to 2017

State	State has comprehensive early learning standards	Teacher has a bachelor's degree	Teacher has specialized training in prekindergarten
United States[1]	44	23	35
Alabama	Yes	Yes	Yes
Alaska	Yes	Yes	Yes
Arizona	Yes	No	No
Arkansas	Yes	No	Yes
California[2]	Yes	No[3]	No[4]
Colorado	Yes	No	Yes
Connecticut[5]	Yes	No[6]	Yes
Delaware	Yes	No	Yes
District of Columbia	Yes	No	No
Florida[7]	Yes	No	No

† *Not applicable. State does not have a prekindergarten program.*
[1] *National total reflects the number of "Yes" responses for each column.*
[2] *California offers two prekindergarten programs:* California State Preschool Program (CSPP) and Transitional Kindergarten (TK).
[3] *In California, the TK program requires that teachers have a bachelor's degree, but the CSPP does not have this requirement.*
[4] *In California, the CSPP program requires specialized training in prekindergarten, but the TK program does not have this requirement.*
[5] *Connecticut offers three prekindergarten programs:* Child Day Care Contracts (CDCC), School Readiness Program (SRP), and Connecticut Smart Start.
[6] *In Connecticut, the Smart Start Program requires that teachers have a bachelor's degree, but the CDCC and SRP programs do not have this requirement.*
[7] *Data on Florida's quality standards are from the 2013–14 school year. However, no policy changes have been reported that would change the benchmarks met.*

Figure 4.4 State Preschool Standards and Teacher Qualifications, 2016 to 2017 (*Continued*)

State	State has comprehensive early learning standards	Teacher has a bachelor's degree	Teacher has specialized training in prekindergarten
Georgia	Yes	Yes	Yes
Hawaii	Yes	Yes	No
Idaho	†	†	†
Illinois	Yes	Yes	Yes
Indiana	Yes	No	No
Iowa[8]	Yes	No[9]	Yes
Kansas[10]	Yes[11]	Yes	Yes
Kentucky	Yes	Yes	Yes
Louisiana[12]	Yes	Yes	Yes[13]
Maine	Yes	Yes	Yes
Maryland	Yes	Yes	Yes
Massachusetts[14]	Yes	No	Yes
Michigan	Yes	Yes	Yes
Minnesota[15]	Yes	No	No[16][17]
Mississippi	Yes	Yes	Yes
Missouri	Yes	Yes	Yes
Montana	†	†	†
Nebraska	Yes	Yes	Yes
Nevada	Yes	Yes	Yes
New Hampshire	†	†	†
New Jersey[18]	Yes	Yes	Yes
New Mexico	Yes	No	Yes
New York	Yes	Yes	Yes
North Carolina	Yes	Yes	Yes
North Dakota	†	†	†

[8] *Iowa offers two prekindergarten programs: Iowa Shared Visions and Iowa Statewide Voluntary Preschool Program (SWVPP).*
[9] *In Iowa, the SWVPP requires that prekindergarten teachers have a bachelor's degree, but the Shared Visions program does not have this requirement.*
[10] *Kansas offers two prekindergarten programs: the Kansas Preschool program and the Kansas State Prekindergarten program.*
[11] *The Kansas Preschool Program requires a class size of 20 students or lower, but the Kansas State Prekindergarten program does not have this requirement.*
[12] *Louisiana offers three prekindergarten programs: Louisiana 8(g) Student Enhancement Block Grant Program, The Cecil J. Picard LA4 Early Childhood Program (formerly LA4 and Starting Points), and Non-Public Schools Early Childhood Development program (NSECD).*
[13] *The NSECD program in Louisiana requires that the assistant teacher has a Child Development Associate credential or equivalent; the 8(g) and the Cecil J. Picard LA4 do not have this requirement.*
[14] *Massachusetts offers two prekindergarten programs: Inclusive Preschool Learning Environments (IPLE) Grant, or the Grant 391 program and Massachusetts Universal Prekindergarten.*
[15] *Minnesota offers two prekindergarten programs: Head Start and Voluntary Prekindergarten (VPK).*
[16] *In Minnesota, Head Start requires specialized teacher training in prekindergarten, but the VPK program does not have this requirement.*
[17] *In Minnesota, Head Start requires that the assistant teacher has a Child Development Associate credential but the VPK program does not have this requirement.*
[18] *New Jersey offers three prekindergarten programs: the Abbott Preschool Program, the Non-Abbott Early Childhood Program Aid (ECPA) program, and the Early Launch to Learning Initiative (ELLI).*

Figure 4.4 State Preschool Standards and Teacher Qualifications, 2016 to 2017 (*Continued*)

State	State has comprehensive early learning standards	Teacher has a bachelor's degree	Teacher has specialized training in prekindergarten
Ohio	Yes	No	Yes
Oklahoma	Yes	Yes	Yes
Oregon[19]	Yes	No	Yes
Pennsylvania[20]	Yes[21]	No[22]	No[23][24]
Rhode Island	Yes	Yes	Yes
South Carolina	Yes	No	Yes
South Dakota	†	†	†
Tennessee	Yes	Yes	Yes
Texas	Yes	Yes	Yes
Utah	†	†	†
Vermont	Yes	No	No
Virginia	Yes	No	Yes
Washington	Yes	No	Yes
West Virginia	Yes	Yes	Yes
Wisconsin[25]	Yes[26]	No[27]	Yes[28]
Wyoming	†	†	†

[19] Oregon offers two prekindergarten programs: the Oregon Head Start Prekindergarten (OHSP) program and Preschool Promise.

[20] Pennsylvania offers four prekindergarten programs: Ready to Learn (RTL) Block Grant, Pennsylvania Head Start Supplemental Assistance Program (PAHSSAP), Pennsylvania Four-Year-Old Kindergarten and School-Based Prekindergarten Program (K4/SBPK), and Pennsylvania Pre-K Counts Program (PAPKC).

[21] In Pennsylvania, the RTL, PAHSSAP, and PAPKC programs have a class size of 20 students or lower. The Pennsylvania K4/SBPK program does not have this requirement.

[22] In Pennsylvania, the K4/SBPK and PAPKC programs require teachers to have a bachelor's degree. The RTL and HSSAP programs do not have this requirement.

[23] The Pennsylvania RTL, PAHSSAP, and PAPKC programs require that their teachers have specialized training in prekindergarten. The K4/SBPK program does not have this requirement.

[24] The Pennsylvania PAHSSAP requires that assistant prekindergarten teachers earn a Child Development Associate credential or equivalent, but the RTL, K4/SBPK, and PAPKC programs do not have such a requirement.

[25] Wisconsin offers two prekindergarten programs: the Four-Year-Old Kindergarten (4K) program and the Wisconsin Head Start (HdSt) program.

[26] In Wisconsin, the Head Start program requires a class size of 20 students or lower, but the 4K program does not have this requirement.

[27] In Wisconsin, the 4K program requires that prekindergarten teachers have a bachelor's degree, but the Wisconsin Head Start program does not have this requirement.

[28] In Wisconsin, the Head Start program requires that the assistant teacher has a Child Development Associate credential or equivalent, but the 4K program does not have this requirement.

NOTE: For states with multiple prekindergarten programs, the table reflects the collective responses for each item. To receive a "Yes" response, all programs in the state must adhere to the requirement.

SOURCE: National Institute for Early Education Research, The State of Preschool 2017: State Preschool Yearbook, retrieved June 6, 2018 from http://nieer.org/state-preschool-yearbooks/yearbook2017. Data Source.

Teacher Tests

After a teacher preparation program is completed at the college level, some states require teacher candidates to pass one or more teacher tests to further demonstrate their knowledge and readiness to teach. Some states have their own teacher tests, while others use a multi-state one called Praxis. In Massachusetts, public school teachers take MTEL Exams, the Massachusetts Test for Educator Licensure, in specific licensure areas. Figure 4.5 details test requirements for each state. Generally, Massachusetts has teacher preparation standards that are equal to or higher than most of the country, and teacher salary in Massachusetts is far above the national average for teachers. Teacher salary is discussed in more detail in Chapter 6.

Figure 4.5 Test Required for Initial Teacher Certification of Elementary and Secondary Teachers 2016-2017

State	2015					2016			
	Basic skills exam	Subject-matter exam	Knowledge of teaching exam	Assessment of teaching performance		Basic skills exam	Subject-matter exam	Knowledge of teaching exam	Assessment of teaching performance
1	2	3	4	5		6	7	8	9
Alabama	X	X	X	X		X	X	X	X
Alaska	X					X	X		
Arizona		X	X				X	X	
Arkansas	X	X	X			X	X	X	
California	X	---		X		X	---		X
Colorado		X					X		
Connecticut	X	X	---	---		X	X		
Delaware	X	X				X	X		
District of Columbia	X	X	X			X	X	X	
Florida	X			X		X			X
Georgia	X	X				X	X		X
Hawaii	X	X				X	X		
Idaho		X		X			X		X
Illinois	X	X	X	X	\1\	X	X	X	X
Indiana	X	X		X		---	---	---	---
Iowa		X	X				X	X	
Kansas		X	X				X	X	
Kentucky	X	X	X	X		X	X	X	X
Louisiana	X	X	X	X		X	X	X	X
Maine	X	X	X			X	X	X	
Maryland	X	X	X			X	X	X	
Massachusetts	X	X		X		X	X		X
Michigan	X	X		X		X	X		X
Minnesota	X	X	X			X	X	X	
Mississippi	X	X	X	X		X	X	X	X
Missouri	X	X	X	X		X	X	X	X
Montana							X		
Nebraska	X					X	X		

Figure 4.5 Test Required for Initial Teacher Certification of Elementary and Secondary Teachers 2016-2017 (*Continued*)

Nevada	X	X			X	X		
New Hampshire	X	X			X	X		
New Jersey	X	X			X	X		(\2\)
New Mexico	X	X	X	X	X	X	X	X
New York	X	X	X	X	X	X	X	X
North Carolina	X	X	X	X	X	X	X	X
North Dakota	X	X	X	X	X	X	X	X
Ohio		X	X	X		X	X	X
Oklahoma	---	---	---	---	---	---	---	---
Oregon	X	X		X		X		X
Pennsylvania	X	X		X	X	X		X
Rhode Island	X	X	X	X	X	X	X	X
South Carolina		X	X			X	X	
South Dakota	X	X	X	X	X	X	X	
Tennessee	X	X	X		X	X	X	
Texas	X	X	X	X	X	X	X	X
Utah		X		X	X	X		X
Vermont	X				X	X		
Virginia	X	X	X		X	X	X	
Washington	X	X		X	X	X		X
West Virginia	X	X	X	X	X	X	X	X
Wisconsin	X	X		X	X	X		X
Wyoming								

—*Not available.*
X Denotes that the state requires testing. A blank denotes that the state does not require testing.
\1\Beginning September 1, 2015.
\2\To begin in school year 2017-18.

SOURCE: National Association of State Directors of Teacher Education and Certification (NASDTEC), NASDTEC Knowledgebase, retrieved July 9, 2016, from https://www.nasdtec.net/. (This table was prepared April 2017.)

Teacher Licensure

A teacher must be licensed to teach in specific grades and subjects, according to the training that the teacher has received. Being licensed to teach is called **licensure**, and it is an assurance that a teacher candidate has fully met the requirements of coursework, practicum and/or testing to teach a specific grade and/or subjects. The **licensure area** is the grade or curriculum area that the teacher has state permission to teach such as music, middle school science, or elementary grades. Some teachers hold licenses in multiple areas because they have met all the requirements for each licensure area.

There are often different *types* of licensure, which designate the amount of training and experience a teacher has. The first type of license is often called an initial license, and it might require a teacher to complete a Master's degree or five years of teaching before being given a professional license.

> **Licensure**—Permission to teach, which is awarded for specific areas after all requirements are met
>
> **Licensure area**—The ages, grades, and/or subject areas that a teacher has met the requirements to teach—E.g., elementary (all subjects for grades 1 to 6) or high school biology (biology for grades 9 to 12)

If a teacher is given permission to teach before all the states requirements have been met, the state usually gives a waiver for a specific amount of time. This waiver can be in response to an urgent need the state has, formally recognizing that the teacher is teaching in a grade or subject area that the teacher is not yet qualified for, or a waiver can be given to allow a teacher additional time to complete licensure requirements.

TEACHER LICENSURE AND TEACHER TESTING

Without a doubt, you'll have to occupy yourself with two frequently frustrating and time-consuming aspects of the teacher job search process: licensure and testing.

Because of the decentralized way we do education in this country, each state has its own licensure and certification process to allow individuals to teach in that state. Several states have reciprocal agreements with one another, meaning that teachers trained and licensed in one state are eligible for licensure in another state. It's generally necessary for you to apply for licensure in the state where you're completing your preparation as a teacher and then, following receipt of that license, to pursue certification in another state. Some states require additional coursework upon licensure. Depending on the state, you may have a probationary period to complete that coursework while working as a teacher. Other states are less lenient, and require completion of the coursework prior to applying for licensure. You should be fully aware of the licensure requirements for your area in your state of residency or the state to which you plan to move. Licensure can cause employment headaches, so inform yourself well in advance, and apply early.

Teacher testing is another area of the employment process that can quickly derail a job search. If you plan to seek employment in another state, be sure to inquire about necessary test scores you may need to submit during the application process, or in the first months of employment. Be completely aware of what your prospective employer will expect and need to verify upon your employment. Again, depending on the district and state, you may be able to complete the testing requirements within a given window of time. Others might require all requirements to be met before offering employment. Know what to expect so that if this topic comes up during the application or interview process you're able to provide an answer that demonstrates attention to detail and wherewithal.

Source: Anthony, Rebecca, and Coghill-Behrends, W. 2014. *Getting Hired*, 56. Kendall Hunt Publishing Company.

Evaluation

Each school district has evaluation requirements for teachers. This evaluation can be conducted through classroom observations and other methods, and it is usually conducted by a principal or assistant principal. In a national survey in 2017 to 2018, the majority of teachers in public and private schools agreed that evaluation helped them improve their teaching.

Reciprocity–Reciprocal (two-way) permission agreed upon by specific states to accept teacher licensure from each other.

E.g., Massachusetts and Florida have reciprocity. Massachusetts will accept teacher licensure from Florida, and Florida will accept teacher licensure from Massachusetts.

Figure 4.6 Positive Impact of Evaluation on Teaching

Positive Impact of Evaluation on Teaching

Area of Impact:
- Helped them determine their success with students
- Positively affected their teaching
- Led to improved student learning

Teachers who agreed evaluation helped them (0%–90%)

■ Public ■ Private

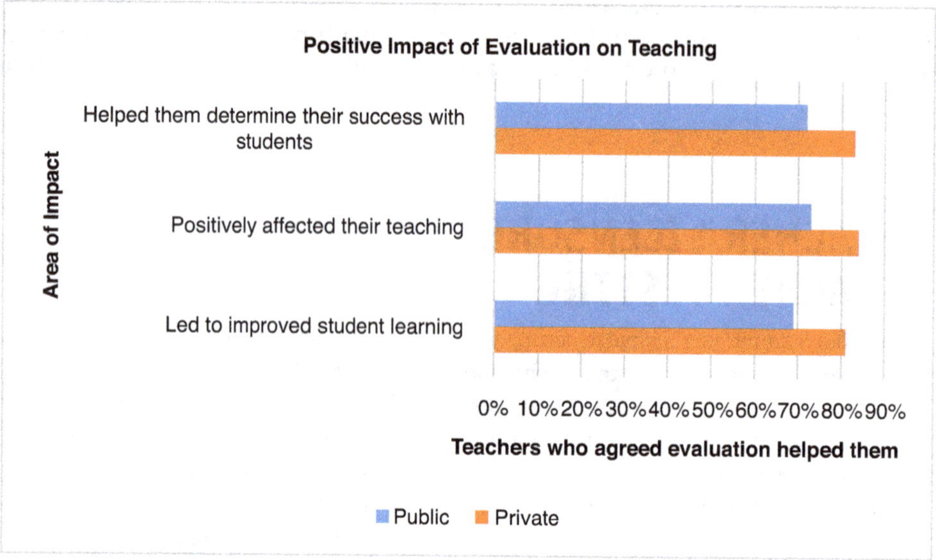

Source: **Characteristics of Public and Private Elementary and Secondary School Teachers in the United States: Results from the 2017 to 2018 National Teacher and Principal Survey, April 2020**

STUDENT VOICES

"The licencing and preparation of teachers is an important part of making sure people are ready to educate students. Currently there are many problems with the system in place . . . like requirements varying from state to state and teachers not feeling prepared for problems they face in classes. These problems must be fixed soon if teacher preparation programs wish to remain relevant."

Venn Diagram _____ SAMPLE-Teacher Qualification for Two States

Name of State A _____ Name of State B _____

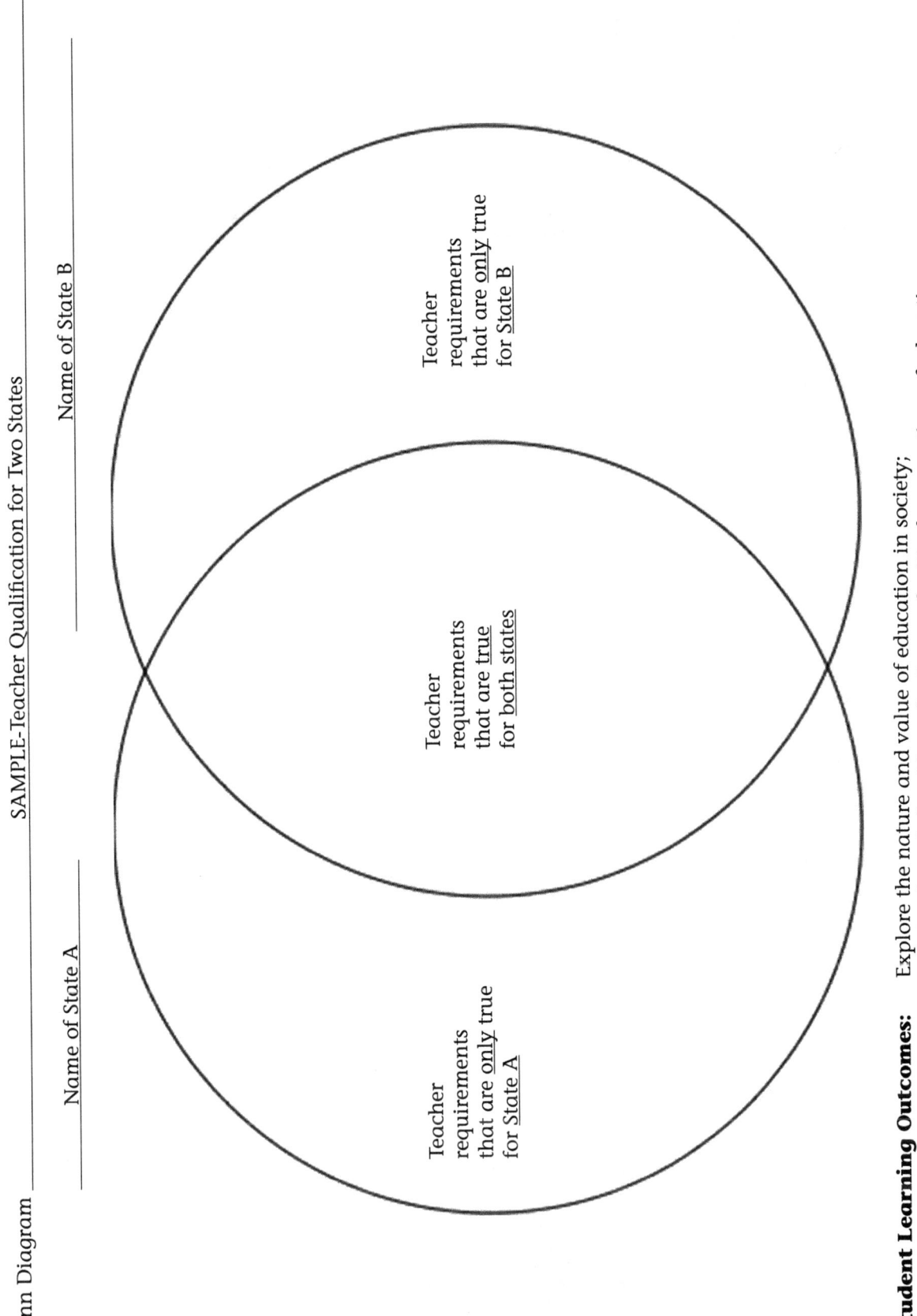

Student Learning Outcomes: Explore the nature and value of education in society; Develop knowledgeable, reflective, and critical perspectives of education

Venn Diagram _____

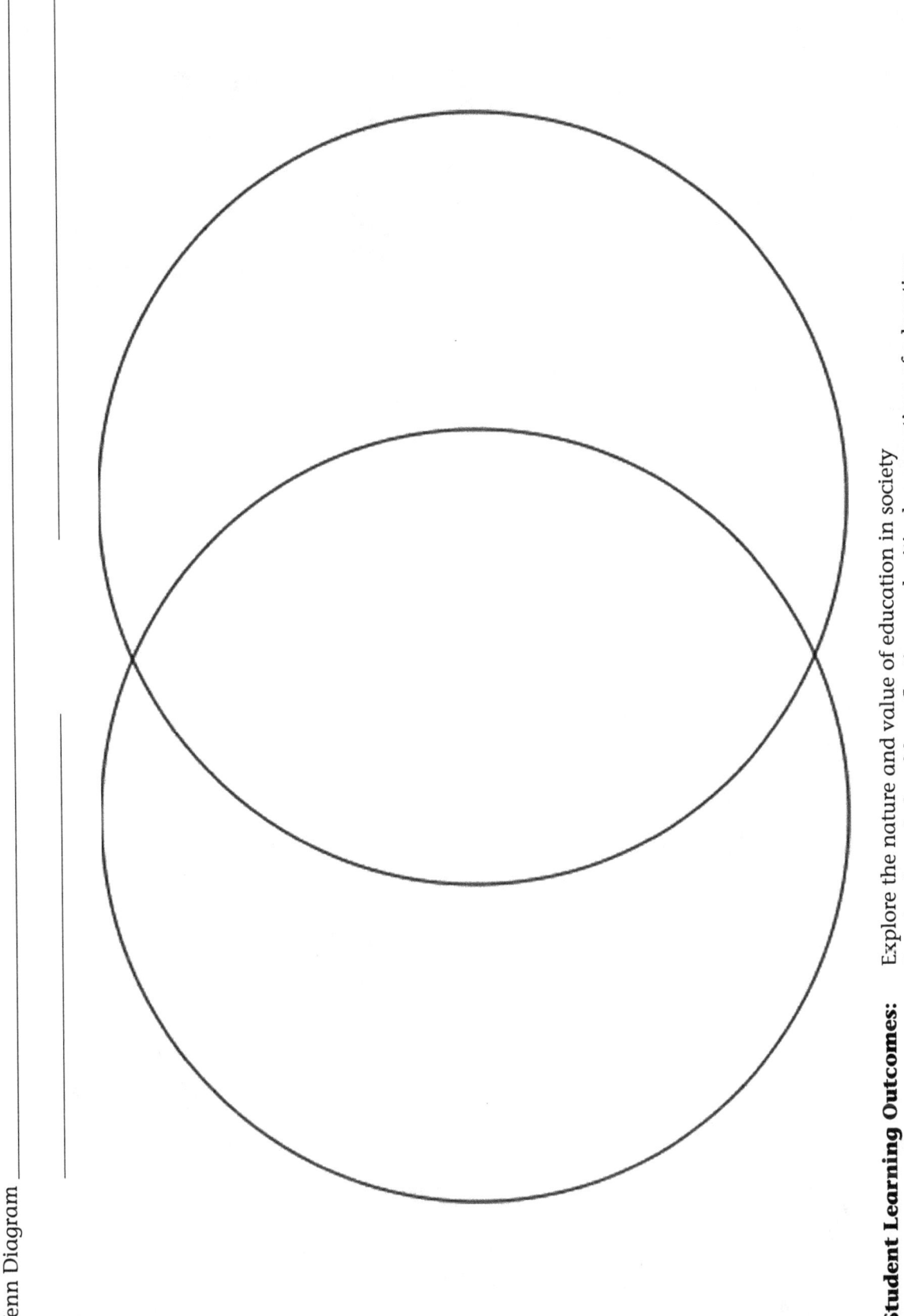

Student Learning Outcomes: Explore the nature and value of education in society
Develop knowledgeable, reflective, and critical perspectives of education

Chapter 4 : Highly Qualified   61

Reflective Writing

Name _____ Due date _____

Required length:

Other requirements:

Directions:

1. Select one of the following figures from Chapter 4 to write about teacher requirements. Which figure did you choose? Circle the letter of your answer.
   A. Figure 4.1 Racial/Ethnic Backgrounds of Public and Private School Teachers
   B. Figure 4.2 Highest Academic Degrees Held by Public and Private School Teachers
   C. Figure 4.3 Graduate or Undergraduate Coursework Prior to First Year of Teaching

2. Tell what you think about the information in the figure. You can use one of the following questions or use another approach in your writing, and you can use the back of this page if you need more room.
   What does the data mean? How important do you think this is? Does this lead to other questions? Do you think there should be a change? How or why?

3. Select one of the following figures from Chapter 4 to write about teacher requirements. Which figure did you choose? Circle the letter of your answer.
   A. Figure 4.4 State Preschool Standards and Teacher Qualifications 2016 to 2017
   B. Figure 4.5 Test Required for Initial Teacher Cert. of Elementary and Secondary Teachers
   C. Figure 4.6 Positive Impact of Evaluation on Teaching

4. Tell what you think about the information in the figure. You can use one of the following questions or use another approach in your writing, and you can use the back of this page if you need more room.
   What does the data mean? How important do you think this is? Does this lead to other questions? Do you think there should be a change? How or why?

CHAPTER 5
Teacher and Student Diversity

> **STUDENT VOICES feature**
>
> "Before now I never considered teacher diversity to be something that may need fixing. I never thought about how many white teachers there are compared to black teachers. I do think it would be better for students of color to have teachers they can connect with more easily, to look up to. But that does pose the question, why are there so few teachers of color? Is it due to the stereotype of a teacher being an old white woman discouraging them, or to schools and colleges often discouraging students from becoming teachers, or perhaps all of the above? Regardless of what the reason may be, that reason should be eliminated if possible so all students can have the best education possible."

Vocabulary

Demographics
Diversity
Diversity gap
Educator pipeline
Parity
Status quo
Teacher retention
Teacher workforce

Objectives

1. Communicate effectively with educational terms
2. Interpret data presented in graphs and charts about the field of education
4. Demonstrate an understanding of education from historical, philosophical, social, and political frameworks
5. Explore the role of schools in maintaining, perpetuating, and influencing culture, both nationally and internationally
6. Develop knowledgeable, reflective, and critical perspectives of education
7. Debate current standards, requirements, and trends in early childhood through secondary education

Teacher and Student Diversity

Looking at the **demographics** of teachers and students in schools today, there is almost always a much larger percentage of **student diversity** than **teacher diversity**. The student diversity is increasing, meaning that the percentage of students of color is continuing to grow, but teacher diversity is largely staying the same.

Students learn best when they can identify with their teachers and when they know that their teachers value their ability to succeed. Students can learn from a teacher regardless of the teacher's racial or ethnic background, but students who never have a teacher from

> **Demographics**—Characteristics of race/ethnicity, gender, socioeconomics, religion, etc.
>
> **Diversity**—Differences within a group—Teacher diversity refers to the different racial and ethnic backgrounds of teachers. Student diversity refers to the racial and ethnic backgrounds of students.

their own race/ethnicity are sometimes unable to succeed to their fullest. Research in Massachusetts has found that "Black boys from low-income families who had at least one Black teacher in grades 3 to 5 were 39% less likely to drop out of high school than those who had never had a same-race teacher" (Massachusetts 2019).

In Chapter 2, we discussed the student–teacher ratio, which compares the *number* of students in a class, school, or district to the number of teachers for that group of students. Looking at teacher and student diversity, we are examining the *demographics* of the teachers compared to the demographics of the students—the percentage of teachers of color with the percentage of students of color, and the percentage of white teachers with the percentage of white students. These comparisons almost always show a huge difference between a group of teachers and a group of students, which is called the **diversity gap**.

> **Diversity gap**—Difference in diversity between two groups

Teacher Workforce and Educator Pipeline

The vast majority of the **teacher workforce**, all the teachers who are currently working in school settings, is largely composed of white, female teachers. The teacher workforce in America is the whole group of teachers working in America, and the teacher workforce in California is the whole group of teachers working in California. If we find, for example, that teachers of color are 8% of the teacher workforce in Massachusetts, that means that of all the people teaching in Massachusetts, 8% of those teachers are teachers of color, but there are 40% students of color in Massachusetts. (Massachusetts 2019).

America needs more teachers of color, and we need to make changes rather than keeping the **status quo**. But how can we do that? There are people in the **educator pipeline**, the steps of preparation to become teachers that include college enrollment, college graduation, teacher testing, licensure, and hiring. But there aren't enough teachers of color in the teacher pipeline, and there aren't large numbers of trained teachers of color waiting to be hired.

> **Teacher workforce**—All the people who are teaching in a district, state, or country.
>
> **Status quo**—A Latin term that means the way things are right now, not making changes
>
> **Educator pipeline**—People who are preparing to teach, who are in one of the steps to become teachers

Increasing Teacher Diversity

Many states and school districts are actively trying to increase the diversity of their teacher workforce. One way this can be done is by hiring more teachers of color. However, the following article, "High Hopes and Harsh Realities: The Real Challenges to Building a Diverse Workforce," discusses how looking at hiring efforts alone will not have enough impact. The authors present four reasons why there currently aren't enough teachers of color for districts to hire. These reasons are listed in Figure 5.1.

> **Teacher retention**—Rate at which teachers are kept (retained) in their teaching jobs, not leaving their positions in a school, district, or state

Figure 5.1 Reasons Why Hiring Efforts Alone Are Not Enough

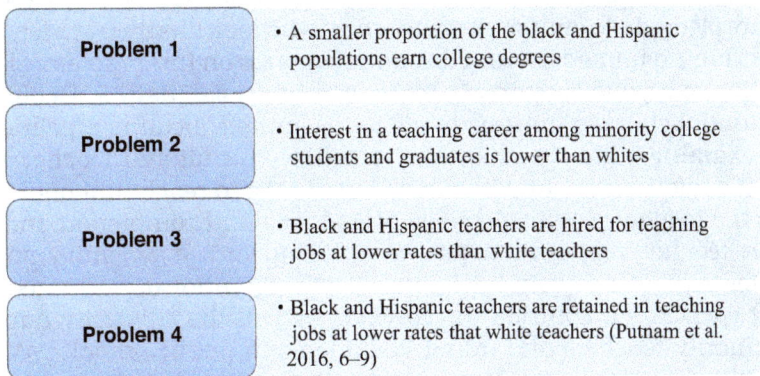

Source: Adaptation based on "High Hopes and Harsh Realities: The Real Challenges to Building a Diverse Workforce," (Putnam et al. 2016, 6–9)

After discussing the problems that are contributing to the lack of teachers of color, the authors of "High Hopes and Harsh Realities" present five possible ways to increase teacher diversity and the likely results of those efforts. These ideas are listed in Figure 5.2.

Figure 5.2 Possible Ways to Increase Teacher Diversity

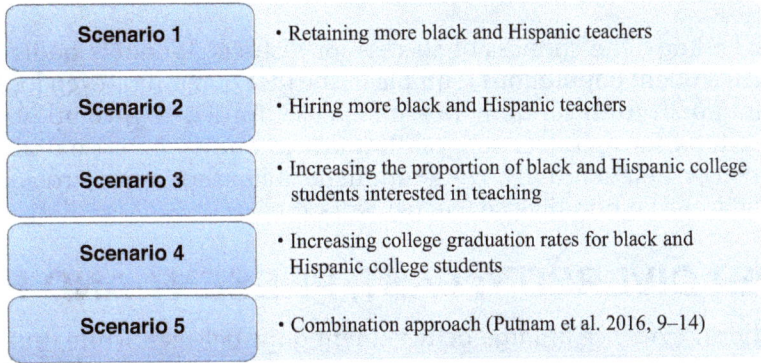

Source: Adaptation based on "High Hopes and Harsh Realities: The Real Challenges to Building a Diverse Workforce," (Putnam et al. 2016, 9–14)

America is in great need of highly qualified teachers in almost all areas. Each school year numerous teaching positions stand unfilled in each state. White teachers will still be needed. Increasing teacher diversity does not mean that white teachers aren't needed, and won't be needed in the future, but it does mean that we need to hire and retain teachers of color at the same or higher rate and with the same success as we hire white teachers. Having **parity** in hiring and retaining teachers of color will help us increase teacher diversity and help provide teachers with the same racial/ethnic backgrounds as our students.

Parity—Similar

In regards to teacher diversity, at the same or comparable rates

[If the headlines are any indication, school districts' biggest priority right now is to hire more teachers of color. No matter which corner of the country (e.g. California, Wisconsin, New York, Indiana and Alabama), districts are pledging to employ more teachers who look like their students. They're supported by lots of well-wishers urging immediate and dramatic progress on this problem. Slate dubbed this "the one cause in education everyone supports."[1] In its own analysis, the U.S. Department of Education concluded that substantial changes must be made to the entire education pipeline.[2]

In this report we examine what it would take to achieve a national teacher workforce that is as diverse as the student body it serves, and how long it will take to reach that goal.[3] We look at four key opportunities along the teacher pipeline: college attendance and completion, majoring in education or pursuing another teacher preparation pathway, hiring into a teaching position, and staying in teaching year after year. We discuss how current and potential minority teachers exit from the teaching pipeline at each point, contributing to what we call the "diversity gap" (the difference in the proportion of minority teachers and minority students in public schools). We then estimate the potential impact on the diversity gap of leveraging each opportunity to bring minority adults closer to the classroom.

Our analysis finds that the effort to draw more black and Hispanic adults into the classroom faces obstacles at every point necessary to become a teacher: while gaps with white adults are minimal when it comes to who enrolls in college, the gaps loom large for each subsequent point described above. These compounding factors mean that the pool of available teachers of color barely supports the *current* level of diversity in the teacher workforce, much less keeps pace with a young population which is growing increasingly diverse and will continue to do so for decades to come. Making serious progress toward a teacher workforce which is as diverse as the students it serves will require exceptionally ambitious patches to fix the leaky pipeline into the teaching profession. As we will show, the path toward reaching a diverse teacher workforce is much steeper than anyone has acknowledged to date.

Given these bleak findings, the chances of success for districts' laudable goals to build a teaching corps that mirrors their student populations crumble in the face of reality—even looking forward nearly fifty years. While that harsh truth certainly doesn't excuse districts to give up and resign themselves to a mostly white teaching force, it does suggest that districts must embrace and promote a range of other, more immediately viable solutions. We recommend some short term strategies that may help to mitigate the consequences of a non-diverse teacher work force.

U.S. TEACHER DIVERSITY: PAST, PRESENT AND FUTURE

Research has long shown evidence of large achievement gaps between white and non-white students in the U.S. One factor that may exacerbate these gaps is the lack of diversity of the public teacher workforce. Educators and researchers have long suspected the importance for students to have teachers from similar backgrounds and demographics, and there is a body of empirical evidence that confirms its value (see textbox). Racial matching shows small-to-modest, but still educationally meaningful, effects on student achievement; consequently, a more diverse workforce could slightly narrow racial achievement gaps.[4]

---

1 Hall, M. (2016, March).
2 U.S. Department of Education, Office of Planning, Evaluation and Policy Development, Policy and Program Studies Service. (2016).
3 This paper takes as given that building a teacher workforce as diverse as the students it serves is a common public goal for all schools. Yet, this common goal should not be interpreted to mean that the goal is for every student to be taught by a teacher of his same race, since doing so would effectively result in school segregation (either across or within schools) and would lose the many benefits of being in a diverse classroom. Rather, we assume the goal is to build a diverse teacher workforce so that all students interact regularly with teachers of their own and different races and ethnicities.
4 Goldhaber, D., Theobald, R., & Tien, C. (2015).

"High Hopes & Harsh Realities: The Real Challenges to Building a Diverse Workforce," by Hannah Putman, Michael Hansen, Kate Walsh, and Diana Quintero. Brown Center on Education Policy at Brookings, August 18, 2016. Copyright © 2016 By The Brookings Institution. Reprinted by permission.

In this report we examine what would be necessary to build a national teacher workforce that is as diverse as the students it serves, and how long it would take to achieve. Starting with the good news, the number of minority teachers in the nation has doubled over the past few decades from about 325,000 in the late 1980s[5] to 660,000 in 2012, the latest figures available.[6] However, those increases have not kept pace with a student population whose makeup has shifted far faster than the adult population. While minority children were truly a minority in the late 1980s at 30 percent of the population,[7] they now represent *half* of the public school student population (see Figure 1). The discrepancy between the total population and public school student demographics are primarily due to two factors:

WHY DOES A DIVERSE TEACHER WORKFORCE MATTER?

As best we can tell, all who enter teaching do so with the goal of being a great teacher and helping all of their students work toward a bright future. However, all teachers carry unconscious biases developed through their own experiences with same- and different-race individuals that may undermine that goal of reaching all students.

Three theoretical arguments have been made for increasing minority teacher representation among teachers, particularly among students sharing their background: more effective role modeling, higher expectations for learning and their future, and fewer cultural differences to effectively teach. Explorations into these theories date back to the 1970s; see Goldhaber, Theobald, & Tien (2015) for a concise overview. More recent rigorous empirical evidence has substantiated the theories that such biases may influence teachers and students in significant ways.

First, same-race matches between students and teachers are associated with greater student achievement. Studies of elementary students in Florida (Egalite, Kisida, & Winters, 2015), North Carolina (Goldhaber & Hansen, 2010) and Tennessee (Dee, 2004) find improvements in math and reading achievement from being taught by a same-race teacher. Effects are estimated to be stronger among low-performing black students (Egalite, Kisida, & Winters, 2015).

Next, same-race teachers are more likely to view students' behaviors and prospects in a positive light. Black teachers have higher expectations for black students' academic futures (e.g., perceived likelihood of graduating high school) than do white teachers (Fox, 2016); (Gershenson, Holt, & Papageorge, 2016). Dee (2005) and McGrady & Reynolds (2012) find that students who have a teacher from a different race/ethnicity have higher odds of being rated inattentive than students with same-race teachers, and white teachers rate black students as having lower scholastic aptitude. A nationally representative study found that black children are more likely to be rated worse in assessments of their externalized behaviors when they have a white teacher than when they have a black teacher (Bates & Glick, 2013). Relatedly, black students in classrooms with black teachers are three times more likely to be assigned to gifted services than those in classrooms with non-black teachers (Grissom & Redding, 2016).

Finally, student behaviors and attitudes are also associated with teacher race. Students assigned to a same-race teacher have significantly fewer absences and suspensions, and are less likely to be chronically absent than their counterparts who had an other-race teacher (Holt & Gershenson, 2015). Students who share racial/ethnic characteristics with their teachers tend to have a more favorable perception of their teachers (Egalite & Kisida, 2016).

---

5 Ingersoll, R.M., & May, H. (2011, Septemeber).
6 Goldring, R., Gray, L., & Bitterman, A. (2013). Table 1.
7 Snyder, T.D., & Hoffman, C. (1995). Table 44.

1) the population of minorities in the U.S. trends younger than the white population, and 2) white students tend to enroll in private schools at higher rates than non-whites.[8] The diversifying trend will continue at least through the year 2060 (the furthest year Census-projected data are available), at which time we estimate white students will account for only 34 percent of all public school students.[9]

Figure 1. Breakdown of the current and projected population by race and ethnicity

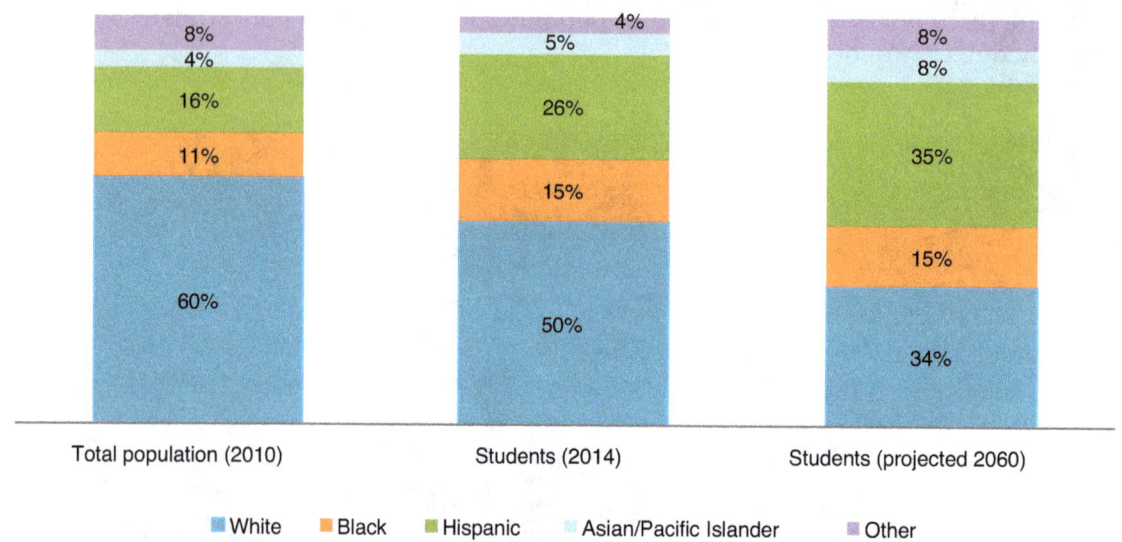

Source: United States Census Bureau, 2014 National Population projections and estimates based on authors calculations.

Attaching some numbers to the discrepancy between students and teachers may help to convey the scale of this problem. The student population is now roughly 50 percent minority/people of color, while the teacher population is now 18 percent people of color. Closing the diversity gap (we refer to this as racial parity)[10] would require about a million white teachers to exit the profession, to be replaced by about 300,000 black teachers and over 600,000 Hispanic teachers.[11] And that's just to reach parity for the current composition of the student population, *ignoring* projected changes in the demographic makeup of the student population in the years to come.

Today's kids will grow up, so eventually the U.S. adult population will also become considerably more diverse, and consequently, so will teachers. But because the student population continues to change faster than adults, it will be almost impossible for the teacher workforce to catch up. As will

---

8 As of the 2011-12 school year, 72 percent of private school students were white, compared with 54 percent of public school students. Bitterman, A., Gray, L., & Goldring, R. (2013). Table 3.

9 These calculations assume the same public-school enrollment rates currently observed by race persist into the future. Please see Technical Appendix for sources and details of the student and teacher workforce diversity projections we calculate and present throughout this report. Note that this analysis focuses on white, black, and Hispanic students and teachers since these groups make up the largest proportion of students; this is not meant to undermine the importance of having teachers of other races.

10 Note that having exact racial parity between teachers and students may not be the goal for all districts; we use this benchmark for illustrative purposes.

11 Calculation is based on data from Goldring, R., Gray, L., & Bitterman, A. (2013). Table 1. In this analysis, "white" is defined as white, non-hispanic, "black" is defined as black, non-hispanic, and "Hispanic" is defined as Hispanic regardless of race.

be clear in the analysis that follows, the diversity gap cannot be closed simply by waiting for more minority children to grow up and enter the workforce.

Based on current workforce inflows (teachers who become certified and hired into teaching positions) and outflows (teachers who retire or leave the profession), we estimate the racial/ethnic breakdown of the teacher workforce between now and the year 2060. Using our workforce model (see Technical Appendix), we depict how the teaching workforce will evolve under current conditions (see Figure 2 panel A), compared against the expected evolution of public school students (panel B).

Figure 2. Diversity of the student and teacher populations over time

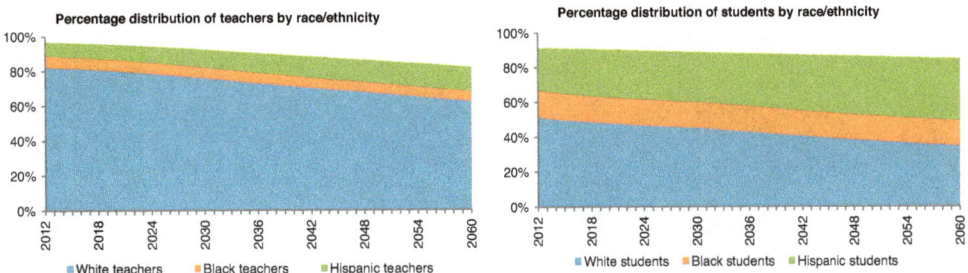

Source: United States Census Bureau, 2014 National Population projections and estimates based on authors calculations.

Figure 3: Racial disparity gaps in 2014 and expected in 2060

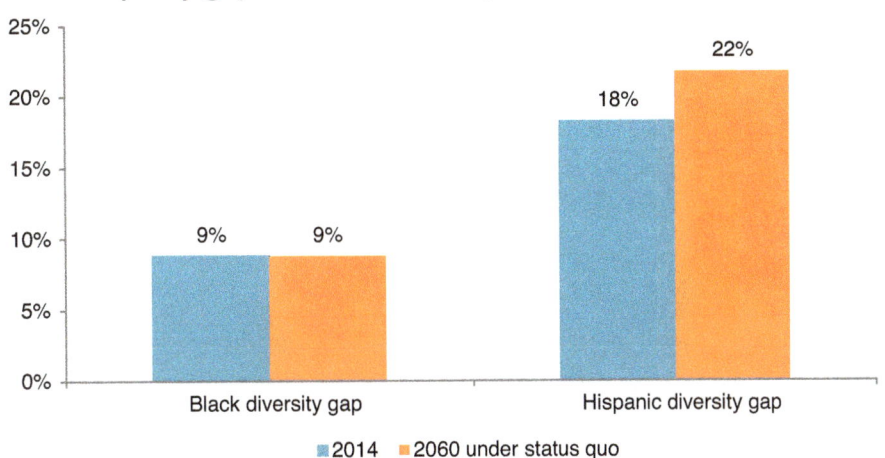

Source: United States Census Bureau, 2014 National Population projections and estimates based on authors calculations.

Assuming we are able to be no more successful in changing current conditions, we expect the diversity gap between black teachers and black students (which stands now at nine percentage points) will remain essentially the same at least through the year 2060, while the gap between Hispanic teachers and Hispanic students (currently 18 percentage points) will actually *increase* by four points.]

"High Hopes & Harsh Realities: The Real Challenges to Building a Diverse Workforce," by Hannah Putman, Michael Hansen, Kate Walsh, and Diana Quintero. Brown Center on Education Policy at Brookings, August 18, 2016. Copyright © 2016 By The Brookings Institution. Reprinted by permission.

Chapter 5 Response A
"High Hopes and Harsh Realities"

Article Sections: Introduction
US Teacher Diversity: Past, Present, and Future
Why Does a Diverse Teacher Workforce Matter?

QUESTIONS

1. Short Answer—Before reading the first sections of "High Hopes and Harsh Realities," what did you know or think about building a diverse teacher workforce?

   It is important and has an impact on the futures of minority students

2. Multiple Choice- Circle your answer. School districts in which part of the country are focused on hiring more teachers of color?
   - **A.** New England
   - **B.** Southern states
   - **C.** Whole country ⬅ *(circled)*
   - **D.** Only California

3. Data Table—Refer to "High Hopes" Figure 1 to complete the following table. What are the race and ethnicity of the percentages in the bar graph? Write in the names of the groups represented.

Total Population (2010)	Students (2014)	Students (projected 2060)
8% Other	4%	8%
4% Asian/Pacific Islander	5%	8%
16% Hispanic	26%	35%
11% Black	15%	15%
60% White	50%	34%

Chapter 5 Response A, *(Continued)*

4. Multiple Choice- Circle your answer. Refer to the first bar graph in "High Hopes" Figure 2, Percentage distribution of **teachers** by race/ethnicity. Which group of teachers will have almost exactly the same percentage of teachers from 2012 to 2060?
   A. White teachers   **(B. Black teachers)**   C. Hispanic teachers

5. Multiple Choice—Circle your answer. Refer to the second bar graph in "High Hopes" Figure 2, Percentage distribution of **students** by race/ethnicity. Which group of students will be a larger percentage of students from 2012 to 2060?
   A. White students,   B. Black students,   **(C. Hispanic students)**

6. Short Answers—Refer to the section titled, "Why does a diverse teacher workforce matter?" to answer the following questions:
   A. How does a diverse teacher workforce support **greater student achievement**? (par. 3)

   Students of teachers of the same race are less likely to be seen as "problematic" or "under achieving" and more likely to be assigned to gifted services

   B. How does a diverse teacher workforce support **higher expectations for learning and for students' future**? (par. 4)

   Teachers of the same race as their students are more likely to expect them to graduate and have higher expectations for them

   C. How does a diverse teacher workforce support **fewer cultural differences for effective teaching**? (par. 5)

   Students tend to view their teachers more positively if they are the same race.

[EXAMINING THE LEAKS IN THE TEACHER PIPELINE

To better understand the source of the teacher diversity gap we need to look closely at the leaks springing along every stage of the teacher pipeline, where potential black and Hispanic teachers are lost while potential white teachers continue to move toward the classroom. The pipeline (for this analysis) starts with the students who are accepted into college and go on to complete a bachelor's degree. The main pathways into the classroom have traditionally been through an undergraduate or graduate teacher training program in an education school, though alternative pathways into the profession are also becoming increasingly popular. All of these routes, of course, require a college degree of some nature. After teachers are hired into classroom positions, how long they stay is another important determinant of workforce diversity. As we elaborate further below, in each place in the pipeline where we can find data by race, we find potential or actual minority teachers who have "leaked out" of the system.

PROBLEM 1: AS MALLER PROPORTION OF THE BLACK AND HISPANIC POPULATIONS EARN COLLEGE DEGREES

This is a crucial obstacle to closing the diversity gap.

Research has long documented the existing racial-ethnic gaps in access to and completion of college degrees.

While college enrollment rates have improved, a wide gulf persists between minority and white students' college completion.[12]

The racial distribution of students who *enter* college looks pretty similar to their distribution in the U.S. population. As of 2012, black people constitute an estimated 14 percent of the American population and also constitute about 14 percent of students who start college. Hispanic populations are nearly equivalent, as they constitute 23 percent of the U.S. population and 19 percent of students who start college.

However, somewhere between the first day of college and commencement, minorities disproportionally fail to persist in college for a variety of reasons.[13] In the end, nearly half of all white 22-year-olds (47 percent) have earned a bachelor's degree, compared with 28 percent of black 22-year-olds and 20 percent of Hispanic 22-year-olds.[14]

PROBLEM 2 : INTEREST IN A TEACHING CAREER AMONG MINORITY COLLEGE STUDENTS AND GRADUATES IS LOWER THAN WHITES

Though college graduation rates drive a deep wedge between teacher and student diversity, it is not the only cause, as minorities demonstrate less interest in the teaching profession generally. For example, students' choice of college major contributes to the gap: a higher proportion of white college students major in education (seven percent) than do black or Hispanic students (approximately four percent each).[15] Though not all teachers going through traditional teacher training programs as undergraduates major in education (e.g., secondary teacher candidates whose major

---

12 Snyder, T.D., & Dillow, S.A. (2013). Table 235.
13 One of the reasons for low college-completion rates among Hispanic students is their lower academic preparation (Cardenas, V., & Kerby, S. 2012). Among black students, their family and work responsibilities, as well as their lower academic preparation and financial constraints impacts their college completion rate (Rawlston-Wilson, V., Saavedra, S., & Chauhan, S. 2014).
14 Snyder, T.D., & Dillow, S.A. (2013). Table 235.
15 Based on 2012-13 bachelor's degree recipients. Snyder, T.D., de Brey, C., & Dillow, S.A. (2016). Table 322.30.

"High Hopes & Harsh Realities: The Real Challenges to Building a Diverse Workforce," by Hannah Putman, Michael Hansen, Kate Walsh, and Diana Quintero, Brown Center on Education Policy at Brookings, August 18, 2016. Copyright © 2016 By The Brookings Institution. Reprinted by permission.

is in their content area), many do, and this provides a good proxy of interest in teaching as a career. Another data point comes from surveys of recent bachelor's degree holders, where 95 percent of white graduates majoring in education express an interest in teaching (when surveyed four years after graduation), compared against 76 percent of black and 90 percent of Hispanic degree holders.[16] Consequently, a disproportionately higher number of white college students and graduates head in the direction of a teaching career.

Other pathways into the classroom, including master's degrees in teaching, also display diversity gaps. We find a smaller share of minority teachers coming to the classroom through master's programs in education than white teachers, as a proportion of the young adult population (unsurprising, given the low bachelor's degree attainment by race).[17] Yet, it's noteworthy that graduate training programs show smaller diversity gaps in comparison to undergraduate training programs.

Some alternative routes such as Teach For America (TFA) have made a concerted effort to increase the number of minorities entering teaching; TFA claims on its website that half of its corps members are people of color. A recent report finds that non-traditional providers recruit more minority teacher candidates (as a proportion of teacher candidates) than traditional providers, 35-41 percent compared to only 26 percent.[18] However, without discounting the impressive success of these efforts, nontraditional providers constitute a small fraction of the new teacher pool, about 15 percent of all new teachers.[19] Thus, though alternative certification appears to be the most diverse source of teacher candidates into the workforce,[20] it is unclear if the recruiting successes among this small segment could be scaled up enough to significantly narrow national diversity gaps.[21]

PROBLEM 3 : BLACK AND HISPANIC TEACHERS ARE HIRED FOR TEACHING JOBS AT LOWER RATES THAN WHITE TEACHERS

While we've identified some gaping holes earlier in the pipeline, the point at which districts tend to focus their efforts starts when they're hiring teachers. This focus is not unreasonable, given that it is within districts' sphere of influence.

---

16 U.S. Department of Education, National Center for Education Statistics, 2008/12 Baccalaureate and Beyond Longitudinal Study (B&B:08/12).

17 Based on data from Snyder, T.D., de Brey, C., & Dillow, S.A. (2016). Table 323.30, 2.3 percent of white adults age 25-32 choose to pursue a master's degree in education, two percent of black adults, and 0.8 percent of Hispanic adults. We do not know whether these people are pursuing a master's degree specifically as a pathway to enter the classroom or as an additional credential. However, based on the data among new teacher hires by race, we speculate that the diversity gap still exists for those who are entering the teaching profession through a master's degree. See Technical Appendix for calculations and assumptions regarding racial disparities by pathway into the profession.

18 Percentages vary depending on whether the alternative program is housed in a traditional institution of higher education or not. U.S. Department of Education, Office of Planning, Evaluation and Policy Development, Policy and Program Studies Service. (2016). Figure 14.

19 Due to confusion around certification routes, different sources report different proportions of teachers coming through non-traditional routes, but the number hovers between 15 to 20 percent. U.S. Department of Education, National Center for Education Statistics, Schools and Staffing Survey (SASS), 2011-12.

20 Bireda, S., & Chait, R. (2011).

21 Another potential drawback of promoting teacher diversity through alternative certification is that alternatively certified teachers generally show higher levels of attrition from the workforce (e.g., Kane, T.J., Rockoff, J.E., & Staiger, D.O. 2008; Gray, L., & Taie, S. 2015).

Overall, we find white education majors are hired at higher rates than their minority peers; this is partially attributable to the lower rates of seeking teaching jobs discussed above, but not entirely.[22] For example, a slightly higher proportion of black and Hispanic teachers prepare to teach but never get a teaching position.[23] This discrepancy could point to a number of potential problems ranging from poor recruitment among minority communities to aspiring minority teachers being lured into other professions. A more worrying systemic cause here could be due to lower passing rates on licensing tests for black and Hispanic aspiring teachers.[24] Importantly, low passing rates may not necessarily imply minorities are weaker teachers, but could point to cultural differences in the assessment or distribution of scores. For example, prior research evidence from North Carolina elementary teachers found Praxis licensure tests signal teacher quality differently by race, with black teachers having significantly lower scores even though there was no corresponding difference in value-added classroom performance by race.[25] Further examination of licensure scores and classroom performance by race is warranted.

PROBLEM 4: BLACK AND HISPANIC TEACHERS ARE RETAINED IN TEACHING JOBS AT LOWER RATES THAN WHITE TEACHERS

Another factor within districts' purview is teacher retention. White teachers stay in the classroom at slightly higher rates (93 percent) than their minority colleagues (90 percent and 92 percent among black and Hispanic teachers, respectively); though not large, these gaps are statistically significant. And among those who have left teaching, black teachers are more likely to report exiting to retire (48 percent), compared to white teachers (39 percent),[26] possibly indicating a more mature black teacher workforce that could lose more numbers in the near future. Similar gaps between white and minority teachers are also seen in surveys measuring teacher satisfaction with salary and how their school is run,[27] which presumably influences minority teacher retention.

Some background information may shed light on the issue of teacher retention across different races. Minority teachers' retention is likely influenced by the fact that they tend to work in schools with higher rates of poverty, commonly in urban settings. The upside of this pattern is that these schools also tend to have higher proportions of minority students – so these students are more likely to have teachers who look like them.[28] In these schools, minority teachers generally stay longer than their

---

22 Four years after graduating, while 19.3 percent of white college graduates are or have worked as teachers, only 16.8 percent of black college graduates and 17.6 percent of Hispanic college graduates can say the same. U.S. Department of Education, National Center for Education Statistics, 2008/12 Baccalaureate and Beyond Longitudinal Study (B&B:08/12).
23 Four years after graduating, 5.8 percent of white college graduates identify as having prepared to teach but have never worked as a teacher, while that number rises to 6.7 percent for black college graduates and 7.4 percent for Hispanic college graduates. U.S. Department of Education, National Center for Education Statistics, 2008/12 Baccalaureate and Beyond Longitudinal Study (B&B:08/12).
24 Tyler, L., et al. (2011) and Goldhaber, D., & Hansen, M. (2010).
25 Goldhaber, D., & Hansen, M. (2010) investigated the signal value from the two components of the Praxis II test and find a small but statistically significant correlation between the Praxis's Curriculum, Instruction, and Assessment score and classroom value-added performance in both math and reading among white teachers; yet, these correlations were not significantly different from zero among black teachers. Conversely, black teachers did show a marginally significant and positive correlation between scores on the Praxis's Content Area Exercises and student performance in math, though white teachers' correlation on this dimension was not significantly different from zero.
26 U.S Department of Education. National Center for Education Statistics. Teacher Follow-up Survey (TFS), Former Teacher Data File. 2004-2005 Table 13. Hispanic teachers report exiting to retire at slightly lower rates than white teachers (24 percent).
27 Boser, L. (2011).
28 Keigher, A. (2009). Table 3.

white counterparts, as their mobility decisions are less sensitive to the racial and socioeconomic status of the students they serve.[29] Yet, these schools tend to be more challenging environments, and minority teachers still do exit these schools, contributing to their lower overall retention rates (see Figure 4).

Figure 4. Teacher race and ethnicity, teacher retention, and proportion of students receiving free and reduced lunch

Percent of students receiving FRL	White, non-Hispanic	Black & Hispanic	Teacher retention rate
0–34	91%	4%	87%
35–49	88%	9%	86%
50–74	82%	15%	84%
75 or more	63%	32%	78%

Source: U.S. Department of Education, National Center for Education Statistics, Schools and Staffing Survey

CAN WE CLOSE THE DIVERSITY GAP?

If we could solve some or all of these problems, could we see a more diverse workforce for the next generation of kids? Are some leaks in the pipeline more urgent to fix than others? Using the teacher workforce model, we manipulate teacher inflow and outflow numbers to "solve" each of the four diversity problems in turn. This model allows us to estimate how the teacher workforce demographics would shift if some solution could overcome each of the obstacles to a more diverse workforce.

We start our analysis at the end of the pipeline with the factor that is conceivably most in the control of districts and school leaders: retaining minority teachers. From there, we will work our way back through the leaking teacher pipeline until we reach college graduation rates.

SCENARIO 1: RETAINING MORE BLACK AND HISPANIC TEACHERS

As described above, black and Hispanic teachers leave teaching at higher rates than white teachers. What would the workforce look like if we found a solution that could patch that leak? Figure 5 illustrates how workforce diversity responds under different hypothetical scenarios. The panels depict the proportion of black or Hispanic teachers under each model; any point where a colored line intersects with the thick

---

[29] Achinstein, B., et al. (2010), Ingersoll, R.M., & May, H. (2011), and Simon, N.S., & Johnson, S.M. (2013).

black "Proportion representing parity" line depicts where the proportion of black or Hispanic teachers in the workforce is equal to the proportion of black or Hispanic students.

Figure 5. Effect of improving black and Hispanic teachers' retention rate on diversity gap

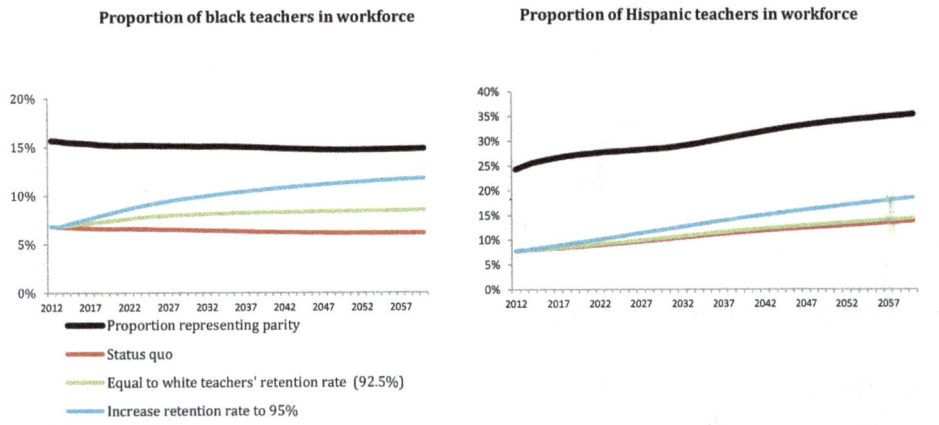

Source: **Estimates based on authors calculations.**

These data suggest increasing minority teachers' retention rate does narrow the diversity gap for black teachers and students more quickly than for Hispanic teachers and students. If districts were to achieve the same retention rate for black teachers as they do for white teachers,[30] the black diversity gap in 2060 will shrink by two percentage points. On the other hand, increasing the retention rate for Hispanics to that of white teachers will barely nudge the Hispanic diversity gap – reducing it by only 0.6 percentage points. In the event that districts could increase their minority teacher retention rates to 95 percent (i.e., retaining slightly more minorities than white teachers), both the black and Hispanic diversity gaps will be narrowed by around five percentage points.

Certainly, this is an improvement (and goes a long way for the black diversity gap), but cannot be the sole remedy for the teacher diversity problem.

SCENARIO 2 : HIRING M ORE B LACK AND HISPANIC TEACHERS

Taking one step further back along the pipeline, we concentrate on recruiting and hiring a higher percentage of black and Hispanic candidates from the pool of qualified teachers, many of whom currently do not teach. This strategy has even less of an expected effect than increasing retention.

---

[30] In the workforce model, we equate retention rates by race. Among black teachers, we also equate those exiting to retirement with white teachers. As Hispanic teachers already report exiting to retire at lower rates than white teachers, we did not change these estimates in the model.

Figure 6. Effect of increasing hiring of black and Hispanic teachers on diversity gap

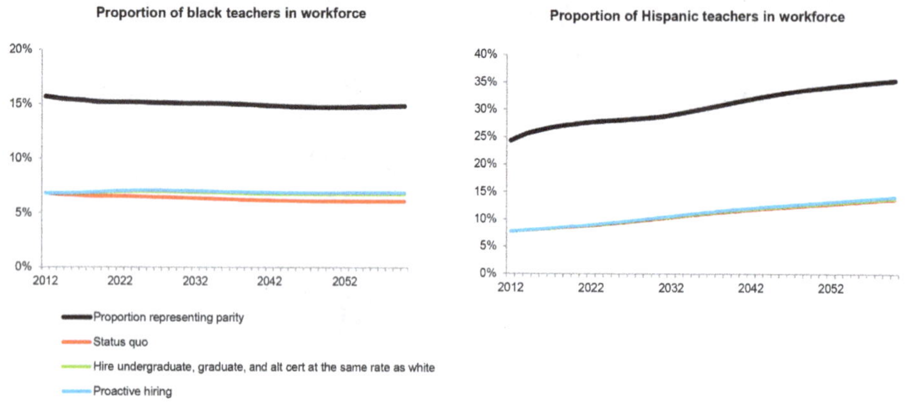

Proportion of black teachers in workforce

Proportion of Hispanic teachers in workforce

— Proportion representing parity
— Status quo
— Hire undergraduate, graduate, and alt cert at the same rate as white
— Proactive hiring

Source: Estimates based on authors calculations.

Unfortunately, increasing hiring from the pool of available minority teachers (all things equal) does almost nothing to achieve parity. Even projecting out to the year 2060, equating hire rates of minority teacher candidates to those of white candidates reduces the black and Hispanic diversity gaps each by less than one percentage point. An even more proactive hiring strategy would make almost no discernible difference (though hard to see, the lines representing equality with white hiring and proactive hiring are almost identical).[31]

SCENARIO 3 : INCREASING THE PROPORTION OF BLACK AND HISPANIC COLLEGE STUDENTS INTERESTED IN TEACHING

Given that strategies targeting only the existing pool of certified teachers will be inadequate, the next step back along the teacher pipeline is to increase the pool of potential teachers by enticing more black and Hispanic students to pursue a career in teaching through one of the three pathways into the profession (bachelor's, master's, or alternate route). We use our workforce model to test a few scenarios.

Reasonable changes to who pursues teaching as a career could make a substantial reduction in both the black and Hispanic diversity gaps. If as high a proportion of black and Hispanic students and adults would choose teaching as white students and adults do currently, the black diversity gap would be reduced by two percentage points and the Hispanic diversity gap by seven percentage points. This seven-point reduction of the Hispanic diversity gap is particularly compelling in comparison to strategies in hiring and retention, which we calculate would make only small changes (less than two percentage points) in the Hispanic diversity gap. A more proactive scenario—in which some unspecified

---

31 In the proactive recruitment scenario, minority undergraduate teacher candidates are hired at 63 percent, graduate teacher candidates are hired at 89 percent, and alternatively certified candidates are hired at 54 percent. The corresponding baseline numbers for white teacher candidate hiring are 59 percent, 85 percent, and 50 percent.

strategy succeeds in bringing in a higher proportion of minority candidates to consider teaching than white candidates—reduces the black and Hispanic diversity gaps by five and 12 points, respectively.[32]

Figure 7. Effect of increasing number of black and Hispanic education majors on the diversity gap

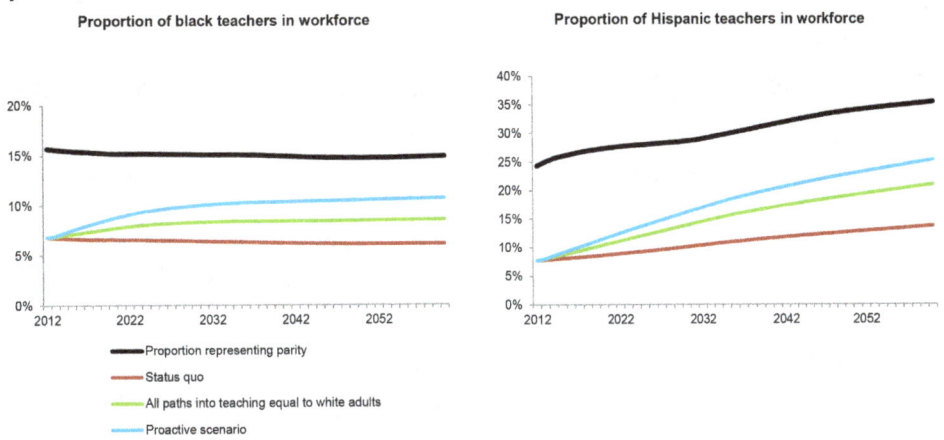

Source: Estimates based on authors calculations.

Despite some potentially promising effects that may result from diverting college students and graduates toward teaching, we must note this strategy is hindered by competing forces. For example, the share of high school students taking the ACT—before starting college—who express interest in education majors have decreased from six percent in 2011 to five percent in 2015 (and white students are disproportionately overrepresented among those expressing interest in an education major).[33] In addition, other professional industries are also attempting to build diverse workforces, hence minority college students may find an education major less attractive than other available opportunities that also place a high value on diversity. Although some minority students may be interested in teaching careers, they could be more attracted to degrees that can lead them to more lucrative jobs in the future including business management, science, medicine, and engineering.[34] Alternatively, minority students may gravitate to other sectors of public service where wages are not high but they may feel they can make an impact.[35] In sum, vying for college students is likely not enough.

---

32 In the proactive scenario, nine percent of minority undergraduate students choose to become education majors, 12 percent of adults age 25-32 choose to pursue a master's degree in education as a pathway into teaching, and 0.23 percent of adults age 25-32 choose to pursue an alternative teaching certificate. The corresponding baseline numbers for white potential teachers are seven percent, nine percent, and 0.21 percent.
33 ACT. (2015).
34 Torres, J., Santos, J., Peck, N., & Cortes., L. (2004).
35 Prior reports have identified a general tendency for minority college students to be overrepresented in majors that lead to lower-paying careers including public administration, social services, or law enforcement (e.g., Allison, T., Mugglestone, K., & Foster, K. 2015); while education is considered a lower-paying field, it is one where minority students are actually

SCENARIO 4: INCREASING COLLEGE GRADUATION RATES FOR BLACK AND HISPANIC COLLEGE STUDENTS

Let's consider the problem that should be at the crux of any discussion of teacher diversity, but rarely surfaces in these conversations because it is also the furthest removed from the teaching pool: the proportion of people who earn college or graduate degrees.

Figure 8. Effect of increasing black and Hispanic students' degree completion on diversity gap

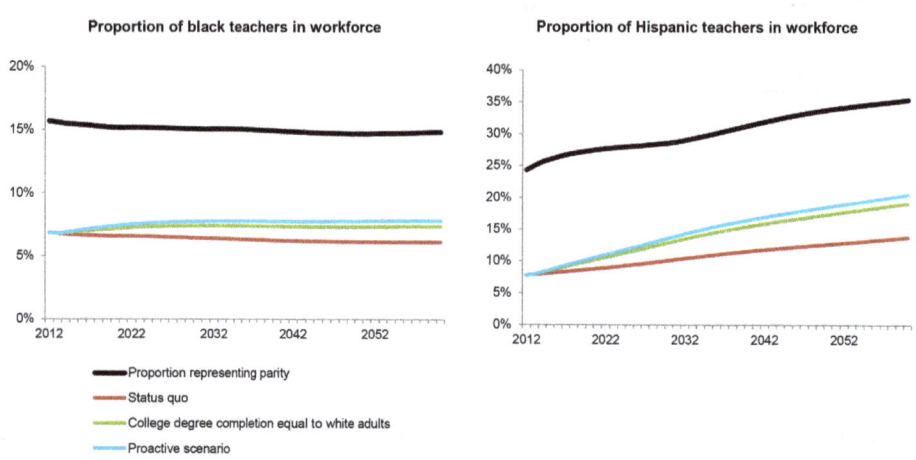

Source: Estimates based on the author's calculations.

If black and Hispanic students graduate from college at the same rate as white students, workforce diversity gaps will drop by over one percentage point and by five percentage points, respectively, by the year 2060. As noted previously, black and Hispanic students enter college at rates roughly similar to white students; therefore, ensuring these students persist and complete college could make a difference in reducing the diversity gaps in teaching. A proactive scenario in which minority candidates are even more likely than white candidates to graduate from college reduces the black and Hispanic diversity gaps by two and seven points, respectively in 2060.[36]

In sum, this scenario is far more effective at closing the diversity gap than a focus on hiring, and is more effective for Hispanic teachers (but less effective for black teachers) than a focus on retention.

SCENARIO 5: COMBINATION APPROACH

No single scenario above achieves workforce parity within the coming decades, but of course pursuing multiple solutions in tandem is likely to achieve greater results faster (setting aside the practical considerations about resource allocations and limitations). The figures below examine different

---

36 In the proactive minority graduation scenario, 54 percent of minority students graduate from college. The baseline number for white college graduates is 47 percent.

combinations of scenarios under relatively realistic targets. In two of the series, we combine retention and hiring scenarios (at the level equal to white teachers, and a highly proactive level), as both of these are the issues that are most directly under the control of districts. The other two series combine all scenarios simultaneously to demonstrate what might happen to workforce diversity with concerted efforts at all stages of the teacher pipeline.

Figure 9. Effect of combining approaches on black and Hispanic teacher and student diversity gap

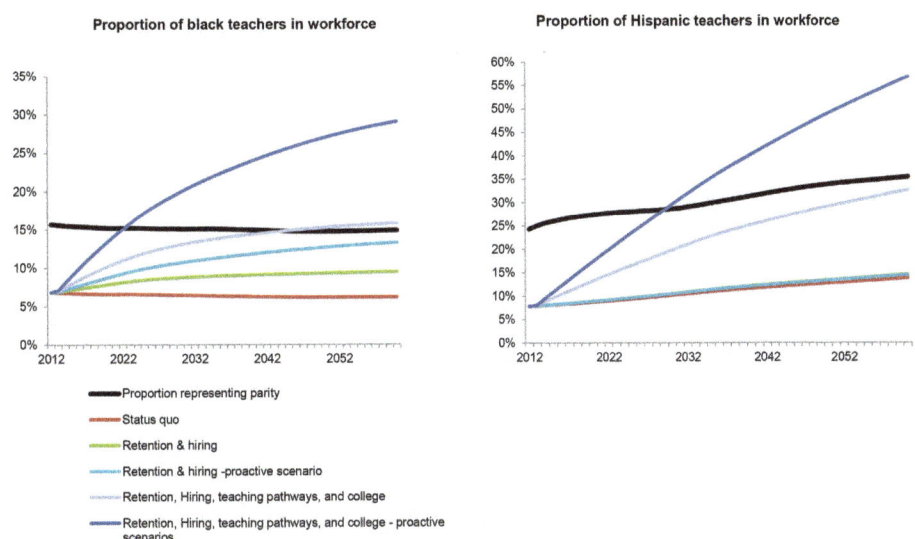

Source: Estimates based on the author's calculations.

These figures show that hiring and retention strategies—those under the purview of districts—could make almost imperceptible reductions in the Hispanic diversity gap, and could modestly reduce the black diversity gap. Moreover, undefined proactive strategies in hiring and retention might go a long way in closing the black diversity gap, but they would make little difference for the Hispanic workforce. In neither case will these district-level strategies alone successfully close the diversity gap. Hence, achieving a truly diverse workforce must include a broader set of actors than just districts.

The scenario in which all strategies are combined and minorities' inflow and outflow patterns along the teacher pipeline are equal to the white adults' inflow and outflow patterns along the pipeline reveals a brighter picture. That scenario achieves parity between black teachers and black students by the year 2044; however, Hispanic parity cannot be achieved by 2060, but comes close, closing the gap by 19 points. Proactive strategies that intend to promote minorities at every point in the teacher pipeline would accelerate the timetable to reach parity, which is calculated to occur in 2022 and 2026 for black and Hispanic teachers, respectively.]

"High Hopes & Harsh Realities: The Real Challenges to Building a Diverse Workforce," by Hannah Putman, Michael Hansen, Kate Walsh, and Diana Quintero. Brown Center on Education Policy at Brookings, August 18, 2016. Copyright © 2016 By The Brookings Institution. Reprinted by permission.

Chapter 5 Response B
"High Hopes and Harsh Realities"

Article Sections: Examining the Leaks in the Teacher Pipeline
Can We Close the Diversity Gap?

QUESTIONS

1. Short Answers—Refer to the section titled, "Examining the Leaks in the Teacher Pipeline" to answer the following questions:

    A. What are two key points from **Problem 1: A Smaller Proportion of the Black and Hispanic Populations Earn College Degrees?**

    •

    •

    B. What are two key points from **Problem 2: Interest in a Teaching Career among Minority College Students and Graduates Is Lower than Whites?**

    •

    •

    C. What are two key points from **Problem 3: Black and Hispanic Teachers Are Hired for Teaching Jobs at Lower Rates than White Teachers?**

    •

    •

    D. What are two key points from **Problem 4: Black and Hispanic Teachers Are Retained in Teaching Jobs at Lower Rates than White Teachers?**

    •

    •

Chapter 5 Response B, *(Continued)*

2. Multiple Choice—Circle your answer. **Scenario 1: Retaining More Black and Hispanic Teachers**—Refer to Figure 5 to answer this question. If the retention of Hispanic teachers is increased to 95%, about what percentage of teachers in the workforce will be Hispanic by 2057?
   A. 8%,   **B.** 20%,   **C.** 35%

3. Multiple Choice—Circle your answer. **Scenario 2: Hiring More Black and Hispanic Teachers**—Refer to Figure 6 to answer this question. If districts proactively hire black teachers, how would the percentage of black teachers in the workforce **change** by 2057?
   A. Slightly increase,   **B.** Greatly increase,   **C.** Stay the same

4. Multiple Choice—Circle your answer. **Scenario 3: Increasing the Proportion of Black and Hispanic College Students Interested in Teaching**—Refer to Figure 7 to answer this question. Which situation represented in the graphs will cause the percentage of black and Hispanic teachers in the workforce to get the **closest to parity** by 2057?
   A. Status quo,

   B. All paths into teaching equal to white adults,

   C. Proactive scenario

5. Multiple Choice—Circle your answer. **Scenario 4: Increasing College Graduation Rates for Black and Hispanic College Students**—Refer to Figure 8 to answer this question. Which situation represented in the graphs will cause the percentage of black and Hispanic college students to graduate with the **lowest percentage** of teachers in the workforce by 2057?
   A. Status quo,

   B. College degree completion equal to white adults,

   C. Proactive scenario

6. Multiple Choice—Circle your answer. **Scenario 5: Combination Approach**—Refer to Figure 9 to answer this question. If a combination of all approaches is used (retention, hiring, teaching pathways, and college-proactive), which group of teachers do the authors predict would reach parity in 2022?
   A. Black teachers,

   B. Hispanic teachers,

   C. Both black and Hispanic teachers

[RACING TO CLOSE THE GAPS

In any endeavor, setting goals is crucial to motivate change. Yet, setting goals absent a strong understanding of what is practical or achievable is less helpful. In this case, the failure to understand both the primary reasons for the scant supply of black and Hispanic teachers and the enormity and persistence of the shortfall have resulted in a proliferation of (presumably costly) initiatives launched by districts, states, and even the federal government. These interventions, while well intended, are all largely blind to the limitations of the available teaching pool and seek to address a leak far too late in the pipeline. Even masters-level initial certification teacher programs and alternative certification programs can have a limited effect, given that they can draw only from the pool of minorities who have successfully completed a college degree. In our view, the fundamental bottleneck here is not so much the failure of efforts by districts' human resources offices to hire and retain trained minority teachers (in truth, changing hiring practices can barely nudge the needle on teacher diversity); rather, the problem comes both from the low rate of college completion by black and Hispanic students and then the inability to persuade them to consider a career in the teaching profession.

The latter problem of making the teaching profession attractive is a familiar one to those of us in the education community. As has been argued many times before, improving public school teachers' working conditions, school leadership, and salaries could go a long way to making the profession attractive to potential teacher candidates.

The former problem of getting more minorities graduating from college will likewise require familiar solutions, and must start long before minority children enter a college lecture hall. And we must continue to support those students for years, until they are holding their college degree.

We must also issue a word of caution about teacher quality. In our analysis presented here, we ignored the issue of teacher quality to look at quantities alone. Yet, we caution against hastily lowering standards in an effort to diversify the teacher workforce sooner, as such a strategy could potentially undermine the benefits of diversity policies.[37] After all, although racial matching with a diverse workforce does show evidence of modestly improving minority students' test scores, teacher quality itself has a much greater effect across all students. A brief on teacher diversity from the Center for Education Data & Research at the University of Washington presents a useful comparison of estimated effect sizes of race-matching versus estimated differences in teacher value-added performance, which shows race-matching estimates to be between 10 and 75 percent of the magnitude of improving teacher quality from the median to the 83rd percentile.[38] In light of these comparisons, we encourage states and districts not to allow diversity objectives to divert focus away from other, higher-leverage efforts to improve student learning, including improvements in teacher quality or improving curriculum.[39]

In summary, achieving a diverse teacher workforce must be a long-term policy goal with a suite of long-term strategies put in place to help minorities succeed in college and to encourage them to return to the classroom to help the next generation of students. Our failure to do so will keep us stubbornly in the same vicious cycle in which low teacher diversity contributes in a myriad of ways to low minority student success in K-12 and college, which results once again in low teacher diversity.

---

[37] This is not intended to imply that all entrance standards are equally effective at identifying teacher quality across all teachers. As described earlier, Goldhaber, D., & Hansen, M. (2010) find evidence of differential signals of quality based on teacher licensure scores, though no difference based on teachers' classroom performance.

[38] The numbers vary based on the grade and subject, and varies across studies. See Goldhaber, D., Theobald, R., & Tien, C. (2015).

[39] Curriculum differences appear to have an even greater potential difference than these common measures focused on teachers alone; see Whitehurst, G. (2009).

"High Hopes & Harsh Realities: The Real Challenges to Building a Diverse Workforce," by Hannah Putman, Michael Hansen, Kate Walsh, and Diana Quintero. Brown Center on Education Policy at Brookings, August 18, 2016. Copyright © 2016 By The Brookings Institution. Reprinted by permission.

The time horizon of these findings demands that even while pursuing efforts to transform the composition of the teacher workforce, policy makers must also consider other remedies that may do much to alleviate some of the well-chronicled problems resulting from an overly white profession. Though fully developing the short- and mediumterm solutions to mitigate the effects of the current diversity gap is beyond the scope of this report, a few come immediately to mind.

First, schools can consider leveraging other staff positions in the school to provide students exposure to diverse groups of adults interested in their academic success. For example, staff positions such as paraprofessionals and administrators, who may come from more diverse backgrounds than the pool of trained teachers, can develop and maintain relationships with students and their parents.[40] Though we do not know of any empirical evidence that suggests a link between non-teacher minority adults and minority students promoting greater achievement, we suppose the presence of invested adults that share backgrounds that match the diversity of the students can only help them stay engaged in school.[41]

Second, district and school leaders should put strategies into place (whether formal or informal) designed to mitigate the possibility of teachers' biases influencing important student outcomes. For example, data from the Department of Education's Office of Civil Rights shows black students (particularly males) are suspended at significantly higher rates than white students.[42] Perhaps a reasonable strategy to avoid suspensions based on biases is to have a diverse group of teachers and administrators be involved in the decision (or perhaps hold veto authority) of whether to suspend a student. Similar review strategies could be implemented when disciplining students for excessive tardiness or absenteeism, selecting children for gifted and talented programs, determining access to honors and AP-level classes, or myriad other decision points. Though this may impose a small amount of administrative oversight and review, the benefits to minority students should presumably outweigh those costs.

Third, we should educate teachers about the effects of diversity gaps. Districts and teacher preparation programs can and should provide training about subtle cultural biases and how they may shape teachers' interactions with students. Although removing all explicit and implicit biases is likely out of reach, educating teachers about them and building their awareness of these biases could theoretically do a great deal to help mitigate them. Existing diversity training, when offered, is often too rhetorical, reflective, and impractical in its failure to grapple with teachers' many decisions that become unconsciously influenced by race. Why don't more teachers and schools systematically examine and react to data regarding the decisions they make, not only the big ones but also the little ones such as who is chosen to be the line leader, or to answer the challenging math problem? With effective training for both active and prospective teachers and a hard look at these types of questions, schools may be better able to provide an equitable education to all students – regardless of the color of their or their teachers' skin.

Increasing the diversity of the teacher workforce is indisputably an important policy goal. Working to close the wide gulf between the proportion of minority students and minority teachers through addressing the underlying issues of teacher recruitment and retention certainly merits the energy of school and district leaders, leaders of teacher training programs, and policymakers at all levels. Some places and initiatives are even seeing small successes in these areas. However, given the magnitude and national scope of this issue, it simply cannot be fully solved through efforts focused on the current teacher workforce – however worthy those efforts may be. The only possible approach to build a teacher workforce that resembles the students of our country is a long-term, whole-system approach that ensures minorities are not leaking out at any point in the pipeline. And truly, the pipeline should start not at college, but well before it. We should ensure all minority students have access to a high-quality education that sets them on a path for success in college and offers them the chance to one day become a teacher.

---

40 Williams, C.P., et al. (2015).
41 It is worth mentioning that as these adults should, in part, serve as role models for the students, schools should avoid situations in which the only minority adults in the school are those in low-skill or low-wage positions.
42 U.S Department of Education, Office for Civil Rights. (2016).

REFERENCES

Achinstein, B., Ogawa, R.T., Sexton, D., & Freitas, C. (2010). Retaining Teachers of Color: A Pressing Problem and a Potential Strategy for "Hard-to-Staff" Schools. Review of Educational Research, 80(1), 71-107.

ACT. (2015). The Condition of Future Educators 2015. Retrieved from http://www.act.org/content/dam/act/unsecured/documents/Future-Educators-2015.pdf

Allison, T., Mugglestone, K., & Foster, K. (2015). Major Malfunction: Racial & Ethnic Disparities in What Students Study. Young Invincibles. Retrieved from http://younginvincibles.org/wp-content/uploads/2015/09/Major-Malfunction_FINAL.pdf

Bates, L., & Glick, J. (2013). Does it Matter if Teachers and Schools Match the Student? Racial and Ethnic Disparities in Problems Behaviors. Social Science Research, 42, 1180-1190.

Bireda, S., & Chait, R. (2011). Increasing Teacher Diversity. Strategies to Improve the Teacher Workforce. Center for American Progress. Retrieved from https://cdn.americanprogress.org/wp-content/uploads/issues/2011/11/pdf/chait_diversity.pdf

Bitterman, A., Gray, L., & Goldring, R. (2013). Characteristics of Public and Private Elementary and Secondary Schools in the United States: Results From the 2011-12 Schools and Staffing Survey (NCES 2013-312). U.S. Department of Education. Washington, DC: National Center for Education Statistics. Retrieved from http://nces.ed.gov/pubs2013/2013312.pdf

Boser, L. (2011). Teacher Diversity Matters: A State-by-state Analysis of Teachers of Color. Center for American Progress. Retrieved from https://cdn.americanprogress.org/wp-content/uploads/issues/2011/11/pdf/teacher_diversity.pdf

Cardenas, V., & Kerby, S. (2012). The State of Latinos in the United States. Center for American Progress. Retrieved from https://cdn.americanprogress.org/wp-content/uploads/issues/2012/08/pdf/stateoflatinos.pdf

Cataldi, E.F., Green, C., Henke, R., Lew, T., Woo, J., Shepherd, B., & Siegel, P. (2011). 2008-09 Baccalaureate and Beyond Longitudinal Study (B&B:08/09): First Look (NCES 2011-236). U.S. Department of Education. Washington, DC: National Center for Education Statistics. Retrieved from http://nces.ed.gov/pubs2011/2011236.pdf

Dee, T.S. (2004). Teachers, Race, and Student Achievement in a Randomized Experiment. The Review of Economics and Statistics, 86(1), 195-210.

Dee, T.S. (2005). A Teacher Like Me: Does Race, Ethnicity, or Gender Matter? American Economic Review, 95(2), 158-65.

Egalite, A., & Kisida, B. (2016). The Effects of Teacher Match on Academic Perceptions and Attitudes. Working paper. Retrieved from https://ced.ncsu.edu/wp-content/uploads/2015/07/Egalite-Kisida-Teacher-Match-Working-Paper-June-2016.pdf

Egalite, A., Kisida, B., & Winters, M. (2015). Representation in the Classroom: The Effect of Own-Race Teachers on Student Achievement. Economics on Education Review, 45, 44-52.

Feistritzer, C. E. (2011). Profile of Teachers in the U.S. 2011. National Center for Education Information. Washington, DC. Retrieved from http://www.coweninstitute.com/wp-content/uploads/2011/08/Profile_Teachers_US_2011.pdf

Fox, L. (2016). Seeing Potential: The Effects of Student-Teacher Demographic Congruence on Teacher Expectations and Recommendations. AERA open, 2(1), 1-17.

Gershenson, S., Holt, S., & Papageorge, N. (2016). Who Believes in Me? The Effect of Student-Teacher Demographic Match on Teacher Expectations. Economics of Education Review, 52, 209-224.

Goldhaber, D., & Hansen, M. (2010). Race, Gender and Teacher Testing: How Informative a Tool is Teacher Licensure Testing and How does it Impact Student Achievement? American Educational Research Journal, 47(1), 218-51.

Goldhaber, D., Theobald, R., & Tien, C. (2015). The Theoretical and Empirical Arguments for Diversifying the Teacher Workforce: A Review of Evidence. Center for Education Data & Research. Policy Brief WP # 2015-9. Retrieved from http://m.cedr.us/papers/working/CEDR%20WP%202015-9.pdf

Goldring, R., Gray, L., & Bitterman, A. (2013). Characteristics of Public and Private Elementary and Secondary School Teachers in the United States: Results From the 2011-12 Schools and Staffing Survey (NCES 2013-314). U.S. Department of Education. Washington, DC: National Center for Education Statistics. Retrieved from http://nces.ed.gov/pubs2013/2013314.pdf

Goldring, R., Taie, S., & Riddles, M. (2014). Teacher Attrition and Mobility: Results From the 2012–13 Teacher Follow-up Survey (NCES 2014-077). U.S. Department of Education. Washington, DC: National Center for Education Statistics. Retrieved from http://nces.ed.gov/pubs2014/2014077.pdf

Gray, L., & Taie, S. (2015). Public School Teacher Attrition and Mobility in the First Five Years: Results from the First Through Fifth Waves of the 2007-08 Beginning Teacher Longitudinal Study (NCES 2015-337). U.S. Department of Education. Washington, DC: National Center for Education Statistics. Retrieved from http://nces.ed.gov/pubs2015/2015337.pdf

Grissom, J.A., & Redding, C. (2016). Discretion and Disproportionality: Explaining the Underrepresentation of High-Achieving Students of Color in Gifted Programs. AERA Open, 2(1), 1-25.

Hall, M. (2016, March). There's One Cause in Education that Everyone Supports: America's Teachers Need to be More Diverse. School ed. Retrieved from http://www.slate.com/blogs/schooled/2016/03/08/teacher_diversity_is_a_big_problem_in_education_and_the_one_cause_everyone.html

Holt, S., & Gershenson, S. (2015). The Impact of Teacher Demographic Representation on Student Attendance and Suspensions. IZA Discussion Paper, No 9554.

Policy Research in Education, University of Pennsylvania, and the Center for Educational Research in the Interest of Underserved Students, University of California, Santa Cruz.

Ingersoll, R.M., & May, H. (2011, September). Recruitment, Retention, and the Minority Teacher Shortage: Fact or Fable? Kappan,93(1), 62-65. Retrieved from http://www.gse.upenn.edu/pdf/rmi/Fact_or_Fable.pdf

Kane, T.J., Rockoff, J.E., & Staiger, D. O. (2008). What Does Certification Tell us about Teacher Effectiveness? Evidence from New York City. Economics of Education Review, 27(6), 615–631.

Keigher, A. (2009). Characteristics of Public, Private, and Bureau of Indian Education Elementary and Secondary Schools in the United States: Results from the 2007-08 Schools and Staffing Survey (NCES 2009-321). National Center for Education Statistics, Institute of Education Sciences, U.S. Department of Education. Washington, DC. Retrieved from http://nces.ed.gov/pubs2009/2009321.pdf

McGrady, P.B., & Reynolds, J.R. (2012). Racial Mismatch in the Classroom: Beyond Black-white Differences. Sociology of Education, 86(1), 3-17.

National Center for Education. (2010). Alternative Teacher Certification: A State-by-State Analysis 2010. Washington, D.C.

Rawlston-Wilson, V., Saavedra, S., & Chauhan, S. (2014). From Access to Completion: A Seamless Path to College Graduation for African American Students. National Urban League, Washington Bureau.

Simon, N. S., & Johnson, S. M. (2013). Teacher Turnover in High-Poverty Schools: What We Know and Can Do. (Working Paper: Project on the Next Generation of Teachers). Cambridge, MA: Harvard Graduate School of Education.

Snyder, T.D., & Hoffman, C. (1995). Digest of Education Statistics 1995 (NCES 95-029). National Center for Education Statistics, Institute of Education Sciences, U.S. Department of Education. Washington, DC. Retrieved fromhttp://nces.ed.gov/pubs95/95029.pdf

Snyder, T.D., & Dillow, S.A. (2013). Digest of Education Statistics 2012 (NCES 2014-015). National Center for Education Statistics, Institute of Education Sciences, U.S. Department of Education. Washington, DC. Retrieved from http://nces.ed.gov/pubs2014/2014015.pdf

Snyder, T.D., de Brey, C., & Dillow, S.A. (2016). Digest of Education Statistics 2014 (NCES 2016-006). National Center for Education Statistics, Institute of Education Sciences, U.S. Department of Education. Washington, DC. Retrieved from http://nces.ed.gov/pubs2016/2016006.pdf

Torres, J., Santos, J., Peck, N.L., & Cortes., L. (2004). Minority Teacher Recruitment, Development, and Retention. The Education Alliance at Brown University. Retrieved from http://files.eric.ed.gov/fulltext/ED484676.pdf

Tyler, L., Whiting, B., Ferguson, S., Eubanks, S., Steinberg, J., Scarron, L., & Basset, K. (2011). Toward Increasing Teacher Diversity: Targeting Support and Intervention for Teacher Licensure Candidates. Educational Testing Service. Retrieved from http://www.nea.org/assets/docs/ETS_NEAteacherdiversity11.pdf

U.S. Census Bureau. (2014). National Population Projections. Retrieved from http://www.census.gov/population/projections/data/national/2014.html

U.S. Department of Education, National Center for Education Statistics, 2008/12 Baccalaureate and Beyond Longitudinal Study (B&B:08/12). Computation by NCES QuickStats.

U.S. Department of Education, National Center for Education Statistics, Schools and Staffing Survey (SASS), Public School Teacher Data File. 2011–12. Retrieved from https://nces.ed.gov/surveys/sass/tables/sass1112_2014_01_t1n.asp

U.S. Department of Education, National Center for Education Statistics, Schools and Staffing Survey (SASS), Public School Teacher Data File. 2011–12. Retrieved from https://nces.ed.gov/surveys/sass/tables/SASS1112_2014_03_t1n.asp

U.S. Department of Education, National Center for Education Statistics. Teacher Follow-up Survey (TFS), Former Teacher Data File. 2004-2005. Retrieved from https://nces.ed.gov/surveys/sass/tables/tfs_2005_13.asp

U.S. Department of Education, Office of Civil Rights. (2016). 2013-2014 Civil Rights Data Collection. A First Look. Retrieved from http://www2.ed.gov/about/offices/list/ocr/docs/2013-14-first-look.pdf

U.S. Department of Education, Office of Planning, Evaluation and Policy Development, Policy and Program Studies Service. (2016). The State of Racial Diversity in the Educator Workforce, Washington, D.C. Retrieved from https://www2.ed.gov/rschstat/eval/highered/racial-diversity/state-racial-diversity-workforce.pdf

Whitehurst, G. (2009). Don't Forget Curriculum. Brown Center Letters on Education. Brookings Institution. Retrieved from http://www.brookings.edu/~/media/research/files/papers/2009/10/14-curriculum-whitehurst/1014_curriculum_whitehurst.pdf

Williams, C.P., Garcia, A., Connally, K., Cook, S., & Dancy, K. (2015). Multilingual Paraprofessionals: An Untapped Resource for Supporting American Pluralism. Washington, DC: New America Foundation. Retrieved from https://na-production.s3.amazonaws.com/documents/DLLWH_ParasBrief6.1.pdf]

"High Hopes & Harsh Realities: The Real Challenges to Building a Diverse Workforce," by Hannah Putman, Michael Hansen, Kate Walsh, and Diana Quintero. Brown Center on Education Policy at Brookings, August 18, 2016. Copyright © 2016 By The Brookings Institution. Reprinted by permission.

Culturally Responsive Pedagogy

Culturally responsive pedagogy (CRP) is teaching with approaches and resources that respectfully represent cultural diversity. This is also called culturally responsive practices or culturally responsive teaching (CRT). Cultural diversity includes race/ethnicity, age, gender, socioeconomic status, exceptional learning and physical needs, religion, and so on. Figure 5.3 shows how cultural diversity can be represented in the classroom through the people who lead the class, through the content studied, through the way the content is presented, and through the way that students interact with the teacher and with each other.

> **Culturally responsive pedagogy**—Respectfully representing cultural diversity in pedagogy, content, and resources

Figure 5.3 Representing Culturally Responsive Pedagogy in the Classroom

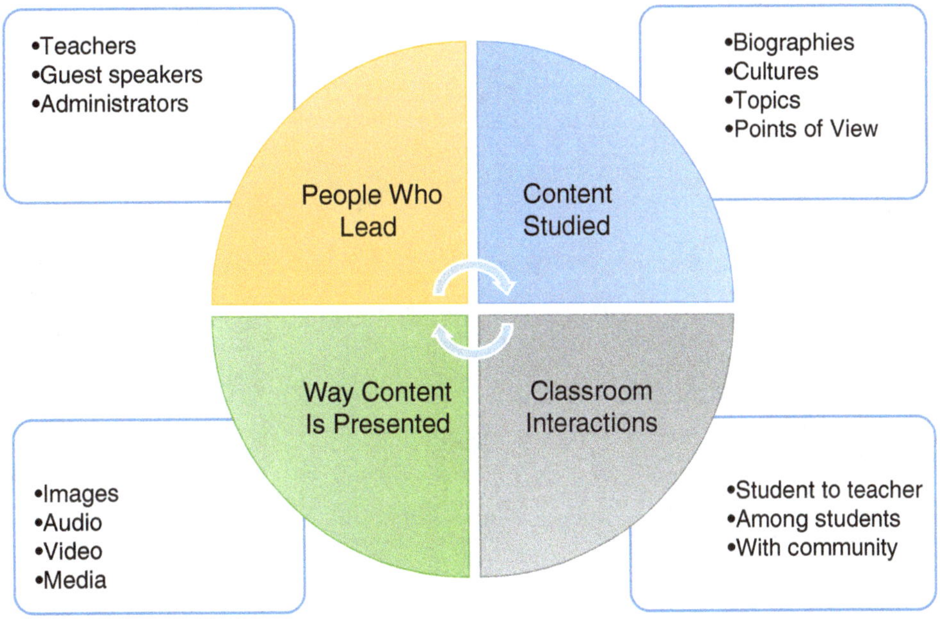

- People Who Lead
  - Teachers
  - Guest speakers
  - Administrators
- Content Studied
  - Biographies
  - Cultures
  - Topics
  - Points of View
- Way Content Is Presented
  - Images
  - Audio
  - Video
  - Media
- Classroom Interactions
  - Student to teacher
  - Among students
  - With community

Source: April Graziano

Students learn best when they have role models and leaders they can identify with—especially teachers—but also including the people and accomplishments they study. Data and research show some of the impact of diversity has on student achievement. Although Massachusetts is number one in the country and world for several student measures, Massachusetts faces "persistent, troubling achievement gaps" (Massachusetts, 2019). A flyer with this information is presented on the next page.

Without CRT, students might think that they can only be like the few representations in the classroom and in society that they identify with, even if those representations are negative. As educators, community members, and Americans, we are not doing enough if all students do not have equal opportunities to learn and improve their lives.

MEDIA EXTENSION FEATURE

STUDENT VOICES

"I think having diversity among teachers is something that is very important. For grades 7 to 12, I went to an international school that not only had students from across the world, but also teachers. All I can say is I wish I had that experience when I was younger. It is one thing to learn about a country, and the people who live there, through watching a video documentary. However, being able to talk to these people and hear their experiences is a gift I never knew I needed. It made me realize just how small I am in this big world. I learned about a ton of different backgrounds, cultures, and customs. I think there is only good that can come from having an array of diversity amongst teachers."

What do Data and Research Tell Us About Student and Teacher Diversity in Massachusetts?

40% students of color

Massachusetts students are increasingly diverse . . . but our educators are not.

8% teachers of color

In some ways, we lead the nation in student achievement . . .

#1
- Advanced Placement success in the country (2017–2018)
- In the world in reading on the Programme for International Student Assessment (PISA) international assessment (2016)
- In the United States in reading and math on NAEP, "The Nation's Report Card" (2005–2017)

. . . but we face persistent, troubling achievement gaps.

But . . .
- Less than 1/3 of our black and Latinx fourth graders read on grade level
- 28% of our low-income 8th graders are able to perform math at grade level
- 1 in 3 of our English learners don't graduate on time; 1 in 7 drop out

RESEARCH SHOWS THAT A DIVERSE TEACHER WORKFORCE MATTERS

- Teachers of color boost the academic performance of students of color, including improved reading and math test scores, improved graduation rates, and increases in aspirations to attend college.
- Black boys from low-income families who had at least one black teacher in grades 3 to 5 were 39% less likely to drop out of high school than those who had never had a same-race teacher.
- Students of color and white students report having positive perceptions of their teachers of color, including feeling cared for and academically challenged.
- Greater diversity of teachers may mitigate feelings of isolation, frustration, and fatigue that can contribute to individual teachers of color leaving the profession when they feel they are alone.

CHAPTER 6
Benefits and Challenges of Teaching

> **STUDENT VOICES**
>
> Teachers' jobs are just as important as any other job. Teachers are the reasons why some people have the jobs they do today.

Vocabulary

Benefits package
Lower secondary

Negotiated agreement

Salary scale
Teaching and Learning
International Survey (TALIS)
Tenure

Objectives

1. Communicate effectively with educational terms
2. Interpret data presented in graphs and charts about the field of education
3. Explore the nature and value of education in society
4. Demonstrate an understanding of education from historical, philosophical, social, and political frameworks
6. Develop knowledgeable, reflective, and critical perspectives of education
7. Debate current standards, requirements, and trends in early childhood through secondary education

Benefits of Teaching

There are countless benefits to teaching, both in the ways teachers work and live, and in the financial compensation teachers receive. Teaching is a great way to take care of a family. Most teachers work close to the same hours and days that their children are in school, so they get the same days off, too. Public school teachers have summers off, time off at Thanksgiving and after Christmas, and most districts also have week-long vacations in February and April. All these times are opportunities for teachers to stay home with their families while they would still be working regular weekly hours if they had different jobs. These lifestyle benefits are also great for adults who enjoy traveling or spending lots of time on other hobbies. There are many opportunities for travel and outdoor activities during school vacations. Another lifestyle benefit is that teachers are lifelong learners. They participate in paid professional development opportunities in their school districts and states.

In Chapter 3, we discussed many ways that teachers get to be creative and make decisions about the way they organize their classrooms and plan learning activities. Another advantage to teaching is that teachers get to work with kids and get to have an impact on their students' lives. Education is a tool that can completely change someone's path in life, which also changes that person's family, and teachers get to be a big part of that. It is a very fulfilling, meaningful job, and many people feel that it's a calling. Teaching takes a lot of work, but it can also be a lot of fun.

Job Security

The financial benefits of being a teacher can include job security, benefits packages, state incentives, a salary that is above the national average for working adults in America, and contracted salary levels. The field of education is one of the most secure fields for employees. No job is fully guaranteed, but classroom teaching is fairly recession-proof because, no matter what's going on in the American economy, communities need teachers to continue educating their children. In addition, teachers earn **tenure**, job security that is granted after a teacher successfully teaches for a specific number of years. For many school districts, tenure is given after three or five years. After a teacher has earned tenure, the teacher cannot be fired unless a serious conduct issue occurs.

> **Tenure**—A job security benefit teachers earn after working in a school district, usually after three to five years

Benefits Package

A **benefits package** is the set of benefits that are given to employees. For teachers, this includes paid holidays, vacation weeks, and summers off. It also includes medical insurance that is partially paid by the school district, and it includes free professional development to make sure teachers know the latest educational research and teaching methods. There can be many other types of benefits, but these are almost always included.

State Incentives

States need teachers, and they sometimes offer special financial reasons for people to become teachers. Some states offer incentives like student loan forgiveness, low-rate loans for first-time homebuyers, sign on bonuses to recruit teachers for high-need jobs, and payment of advanced college degrees and/or on-the-job training for high-need administrative positions.

Teacher Salary

It is common knowledge that teachers are not paid well for the levels of college they complete. That same amount of college could be used to earn far higher salaries in other fields. However, what is not commonly known is that many teachers make higher salaries than the national averages for working adults (Figure 6.1).

Figure 6.1 Average Base Salaries of Public and Private School Teachers, 2017 to 2018

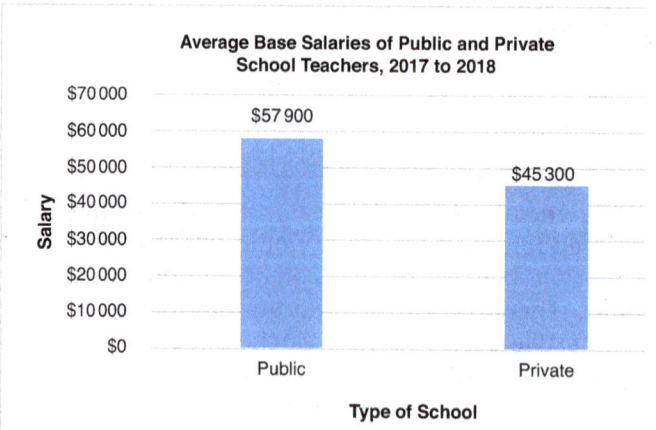

Source: Characteristics of Public and Private Elementary and Secondary School Teachers in the United States: Results from the 2017 to 2018 National Teacher and Principal Survey, April 2020

Note: Base salary is the contracted annual salary. It does not include extra earning for other work such as summer school or other out-of-school-time contracts.

Salary Schedule

Salaries for public school teachers are determined by a negotiated agreement salary scale. A **negotiated agreement** is a contract reached between a school district and the teachers' union in that district. A **salary scale** is a table of salary levels for teachers, based on the number of years a teacher has worked in the district (on the left side) and the teacher's highest degree (across the top). Each district has its own teacher contract and salary scale.

The example in Figure 6.2 shows a salary scale from 201x to 201x (e.g., the years 2015–2017). In the following table, a new teacher with no full-time teaching experience and a Bachelor's degree would make $39,480 for the first year. A teacher in the same district who has a Bachelor's degree and 10 years' experience would make $58,030 for that year. A teacher with a Master's degree and 10 years' experience would make $62,380 under that negotiate

> **Negotiated agreement**—A contract between two groups
>
> **Salary scale**—A detailed table that outlines the salaries for people working under that contract

Figure 6.2 Negotiated Agreement Salary Scale

NEGOTIATED AGREEMENT SALARY SCALE 201X-201X					
YEAR/STEP	B	B+15	B+30/M	M+15	M+30
1	39480	41460	43820	46190	49350
2	41460	43430	45800	48170	51320
3	43430	45400	47770	50140	53300
4	45400	47380	49750	52110	55270
5	47380	49350	51720	54090	57250
6	49350	51720	53690	56060	59610
7	51720	53690	56060	58430	61590
8	53690	56060	58030	60400	63960
9	56060	58030	60400	62770	65930
10	58030	60010	62380	64750	68300
11	61190	63170	65540	67900	71460
12	64350	66330	68690	71060	74620
13	64850	66830	71250	72220	76270
14	65350	67330	71900	72870	76930
15	65850	67830	72560	73530	77480
16	66350	68330	73120	74000	77940
17	66850	68830	73770	74640	78500
18	67350	69330	74270	75240	79000
19	67830	69800	74930	75800	79550
20	68330	70300	75430	76400	80150
21	68690	70870	75410	76980	80630
22	69390	71270	75910	77380	81330
23	70370	71850	76380	77750	81800
24	70670	72350	76880	78350	82300
25	72640	73830	77350	78720	82970

The first column (year/step) corresponds to the "years of teaching" a candidate has accumulated. Pre-service teaching assignments are not generally considered when calculating years of service, although some districts do consider professional experience in the content area, or related teaching experiences when placing candidates on the salary scale. The letter B refers to Bachelor's Degree and the M refers to Master's Degree. The (+15, 30) that follows refers to number of credit hours beyond the degree.

Source: Anthony, R., and Coghill-Behrends, W. 2014. *Getting Hired.* Kendall Hunt Publishing Company. 147.

agreement. Each year, a teacher gains one more year of experience, so the teacher moves down one step on the salary scale, increasing the salary. When teachers complete additional training through graduate courses and/or degrees, they move to the right to the column for their highest level of training. The details will change from district to district, but almost all teacher salaries work this way.

In addition to the amount of experience and level of degree, teacher salaries are also different depending on the type of educational setting. Figure 6.3 shows that the average salary in 2017 for public school teachers was $57,900 and for private school teachers was $45,300. Most public school teachers make more than the national average salary for all U.S. jobs, which was $50,322 in 2017. The average salary for Massachusetts public school teachers was considerably higher at $81,070 that year.

Figure 6.3 Comparison of Average Annual Salaries—Teachers and US Average for All Jobs

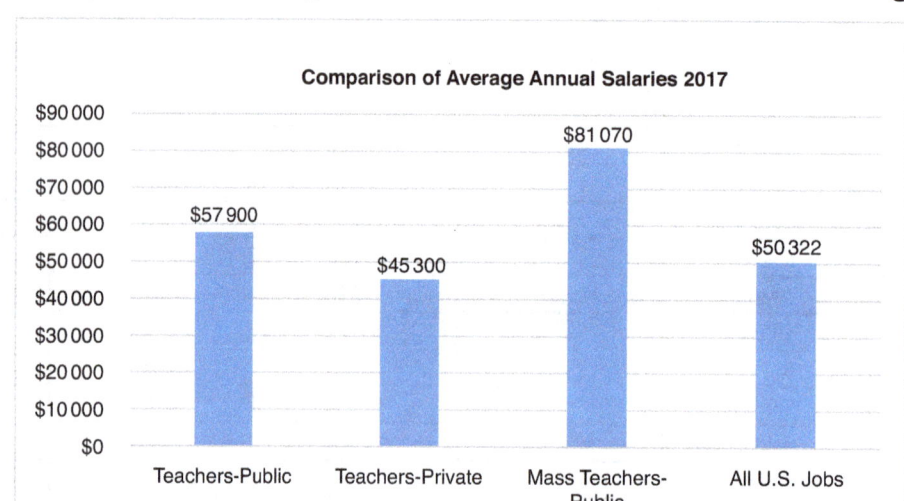

Source: (a) Characteristics of Public and Private Elementary and Secondary School Teachers in the United States: Results from the 2017 to 2018 National Teacher and Principal Survey, April 2020; (b) National Average Wage Indexing Series, 1951 to 2018.

Data from the National Education Association (NEA) for 2017 shows that the top five average salaries are considerably higher than the national average teacher salary (Figure 6.4). New York had the highest average in the country at $79,637, followed by California ($78,711), Massachusetts ($77,804), the District of Columbia ($76,131), and Connecticut ($72,561). A table of average teacher salaries by state is included at the end of this chapter.

Figure 6.4 Top Five Average Teacher Salaries in the United States

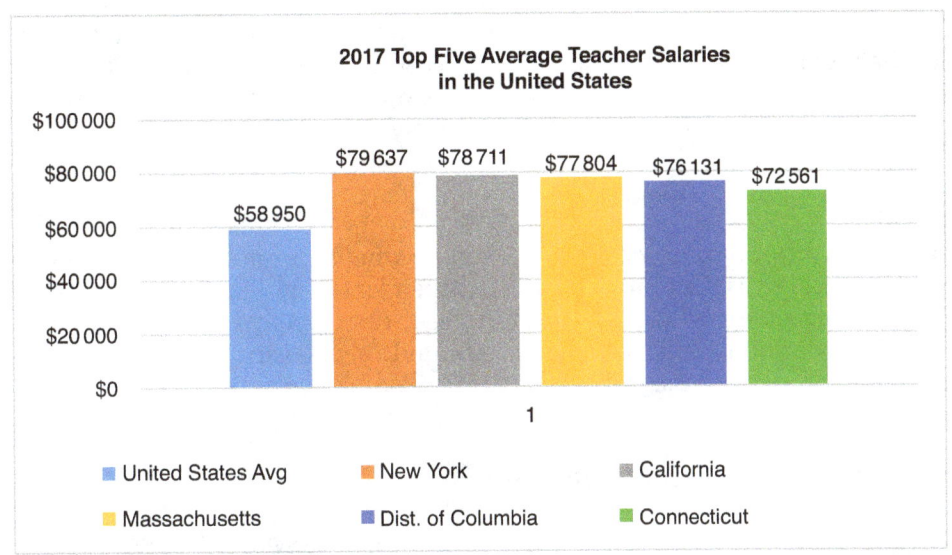

Source: National Education Association, Estimates of School Statistics, selected years, 1969 to 1970 through 2016 to 2017 (August 2017).

MEDIA EXTENSION FEATURE

"Are Teachers Valued as Professionals?" (2:36)

https://www.youtube.com/watch?v=Jc7A3uvAas0

Results from TALIS are summarized in an animated video that asks questions about how to improve teaching as a career choice. Watch this brief video for a glance at issues surrounding how society views teaching.

Comparison of American and International Teachers

Not all countries require mandatory school for children, and some countries only provide high school equivalent education for advanced-performing students. For these reasons, comparing the grades before high school (middle and junior high school) allows for wider participation in international surveys. This prehigh school level is called **lower secondary** for comparing educational systems in different parts of the world. The Teaching and Learning International Survey (**TALIS**) is an annual survey that is useful in comparing characteristics of teachers in America and teachers in educational systems in other countries or territories.

Salary Satisfaction

In the United States, 41% of lower secondary teachers and principals responded that they "agree" or "strongly agree" that they were satisfied with their salaries. The average for all TALIS responders was slightly lower at 39% (TALIS, p.23).

Job Satisfaction and Value in Society

There is a large difference between the percentage of lower secondary teachers in the United States who are happy in their jobs and the percentage who think society values teachers. Although 90% of all US teachers and principals "agreed" or "strongly agreed" that they were happy with their jobs, only 36% of US teachers "agreed" or "strongly agreed" that society values teaching (TALIS, p. 15).

Autonomy

Another way to measure job satisfaction is to examine whether or not teachers feel that they are able to do their jobs. Autonomy is the ability to work independently, making your own decisions. Figure 6.5 illustrates that the vast majority of US teachers "agreed" or "strongly agreed" that they had autonomy in three areas of responsibility: selecting teaching materials, assessing student needs, and determining the amount of homework they assigned.

Figure 6.5 Areas of US Teacher Autonomy

96%	• Feel they have control selecting classroom teachomg materials
93%	• Feel they have control assessing students needs
91%	• Feel they have control determining the amount of homework

Source: April Graziano using data from TALIS, 2018, p. 27

Challenges of Teaching

Teaching is very time-consuming and stressful. Although teachers have regular vacations and holidays, they have many responsibilities on the job. Teachers also bring work home with them in the afternoons and on weekends to grade student work and plan lessons. According to the 2018 TALIS results, US teachers spent more time on the job than teachers in most parts of the world. US teachers spent an average of 28 hours teaching and an additional 18 hours on other tasks, totaling 46 hours per week. Teachers from only two educational systems, Japan and Kazakhstan, reported working more hours per week than US teachers.

Sources of Stress

Teaching is a very stressful job, partially because a teacher is continually making decisions. Even while teaching, a teacher makes decisions based on how students respond to the lesson, how students behave, whether or not they should change the teaching approach, monitoring noises and nearby groups, gaging the amount of time needed for everything that is done, and responding to interruptions from outside the classroom. In addition, teachers often have to respond to emotional situations. Figure 6.6 illustrates the percentage of US middle and junior high school teachers who responded that responsibilities listed in the figure caused "quite a bit" or "a lot" of stress in their work.

Figure 6.6 Sources of Stress for Teachers

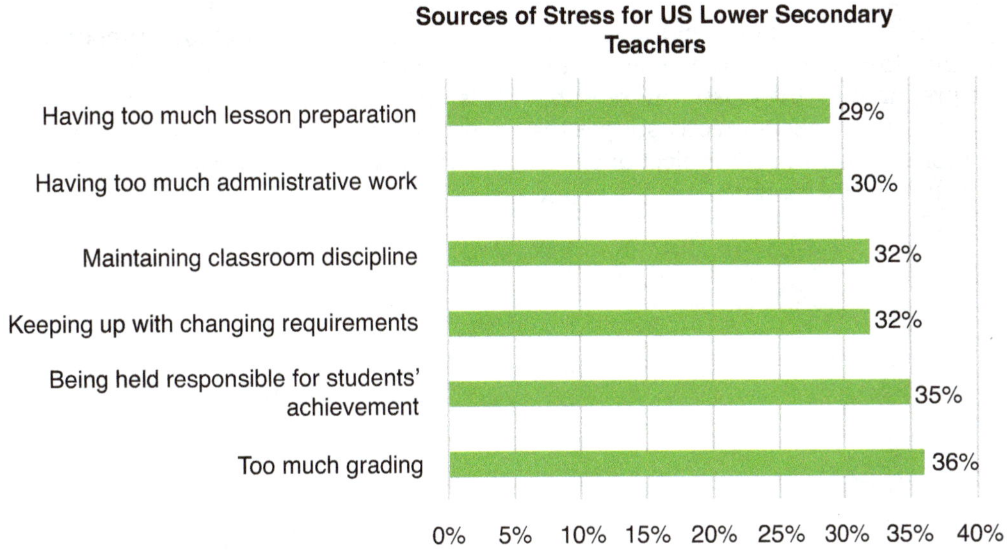

Sources of Stress for US Lower Secondary Teachers

- Having too much lesson preparation: 29%
- Having too much administrative work: 30%
- Maintaining classroom discipline: 32%
- Keeping up with changing requirements: 32%
- Being held responsible for students' achievement: 35%
- Too much grading: 36%

Source: Teaching and Learning International Survey, 2018, p. 21

Additional Challenges

Along with the challenges listed above that teachers face in the classroom they also have to be prepared for violence in schools, including bullying, community violence, and school shootings. Each of these issues will be explored further in the course.

MEDIA EXTENSION FEATURE

Should school shootings be part of pop culture?

CNN news segment, "Brand Sparks Outrage Over School Shooting-Themed Hoodies"

https://www.cnn.com/videos/fashion/2019/09/18/bstroy-school-shooting-hoodies-backlash-mxp-vpx.hln (1:31) 9/18/19

Arming Teachers

There continue to be school shootings, and there are several ideas about possibly **arming teachers** so they have guns in case a shooter enters their schools. However, there are many questions surrounding arming teachers, whether or not you agree that this is a solution to protect students. When thinking about this topic, consider other questions that should be answered, and remember that this is a very complex and emotional issue. No part of this topic is a simple yes/no argument. Put yourself in the place of a teacher with a gun in the classroom, as a teacher next door to another teacher who has a gun, as a student in the classroom, as a parent, and so on. Considering this topic from several viewpoints will help you see the many complex facets of the issue.

Arming teachers— Giving guns to some or all teachers to help protect students

> **STUDENT VOICES**
>
> "One requirement for Teacher Preparation I think is very important is actually preparing the teacher for the classroom, as many studies have found that after the programs the teachers were left very unprepared for the classroom setting. This is very important to me because no matter how hard you try, the teacher really shapes the environment of the classroom. I have always succeeded more greatly in any subject or classroom that has a good environment and a well prepared, well-rounded teacher."

United States Average	**$58,950**
New York	79,637
California	78,711
Massachusetts	77,804
Dist. of Columbia	76,131
Connecticut	72,561
New Jersey	69,623
Alaska	68,138
Maryland	66,961
Rhode Island	66,477
Pennsylvania	65,863
Michigan	62,200
Oregon	61,631
Illinois	61,602
Delaware	60,214
Vermont	60,187
Wyoming	58,650
Hawaii	57,674
Nevada	57,376
Minnesota	57,346
New Hampshire	57,253
Ohio	57,000
Iowa	55,443
Wisconsin	54,998
Georgia	54,602
Washington	54,147
Texas	52,575
Kentucky	52,339
Nebraska	52,338
North Dakota	51,618
Montana	51,422
Maine	51,077
Virginia	51,049

Indiana	50,554
Louisiana	50,000
North Carolina	49,837
Florida	49,407
Alabama	48,868
Arkansas	48,616
South Carolina	48,598
Tennessee	48,456
Missouri	48,293
Kansas	47,984
Idaho	47,504
New Mexico	47,500
Arizona	47,403
Utah	47,244
Colorado	46,506
West Virginia	45,701
Oklahoma	45,245
Mississippi	42,925
South Dakota	42,668

Source: National Education Association, Estimates of School Statistics, selected years, 1969 to 1970 through 2016 to 2017. (This table was prepared August 2017.)

Chapter 6 Reflective Writing

Name _____ Due date _____

Required length:

Other requirements:

Directions:

1. Select one of the figures from Chapter 6 to write benefits of teaching. Circle your answer.
   Figure 6.1 Average Base Salary of Public and Private School Teachers, 2017 to 2018
   Figure 6.2 Negotiated Agreement Salary Scale, 201× to 201×
   Figure 6.3 Comparison of Average Annual Salaries—Teachers and US Average for All Jobs
   Figure 6.4 Top Five Average Teacher Salaries in the United States
   Figure 6.5 Areas of US Teacher Autonomy

2. Tell what you think about the information in the figure. You can use one of the following questions or use another approach in your writing, and you can use the back of this page if you need more room.
   What does the data mean? How important do you think this is? Does this lead to other questions? Do you think there should be a change? How or why?

3. Select one of the sources of stress from Figure 6.6.
   Write down the source you chose:
   Tell what you think this about information. You can use one of the following questions or use another approach in your writing, and you can use the back of this page if you need more room.
   What does the data mean? How important do you think this is? Does this lead to other questions? Do you think there should be a change? How or why?

Section II – Interview

Name _____ Due date _____

Required length:

Other requirements:

Directions:

1. **Getting started**
   Arrange a time to interview an educator, family member, or other community member about the field of education. Here are some ideas to help you get started:

Educator	Family member
School administrator	Student
Staff member	Business owner
Legislator	Other community member

2. **Information about the person you interviewed**

   What is the name of the person you interviewed, and how are they involved in education? Where did the interview take place?
   Date:

3. **Interview questions**
   Prepare some interview questions ahead of time and write them down. You can use the back of this worksheet to create your own questions or take notes.

   A. What type of school did/do you attend, and what was/is it like?

   B. Are there grades or levels of education that you are most familiar with?

   C. What is something that you think is good about education today?

   D. If you could change one thing about American education, what would it be?

   E. Would you recommend a friend or family member to become a teacher? Why/why not?

   F. What years of education do you think are the most important for a student?

G. What idea would you want to include if you could design the perfect school?

H. Do you think school funding or teacher salaries should be increased? Why/why not?

I. If you had a favorite teacher in school, what was that teacher like?

4. Write two or more paragraphs to discuss this interview. You can describe how the interview went, things that surprised you, answers that you agreed with or disagreed with, and other ideas to show what you learned about education from this interview.

Name _____   Due Date _____

Section II—Issues and Trends in Education

Directions

1) Consider the educational issues and trends that were discussed in Section II. Think about the arguments related to each issue, and then show how much you disagree or agree by placing that issue on the following line:
   Arming Teachers—Teachers should carry weapons in school to protect students.
   Class Size—Smaller class size is better for students and teachers in the long term.
   No-Zero Grading Policy—Teachers should be able to give a zero as a grade.
   Teacher Preparation—The coursework and other requirements for teachers should not change.
   Teacher Diversity—School districts' efforts are enough to diversify the teacher workforce.
   Teacher Salary—Teacher salaries should be similar to other jobs that have the same degrees.

2) Place a dot on the diagram for each item and label the items.

Disagree   **Agree**

100%   50%   100%

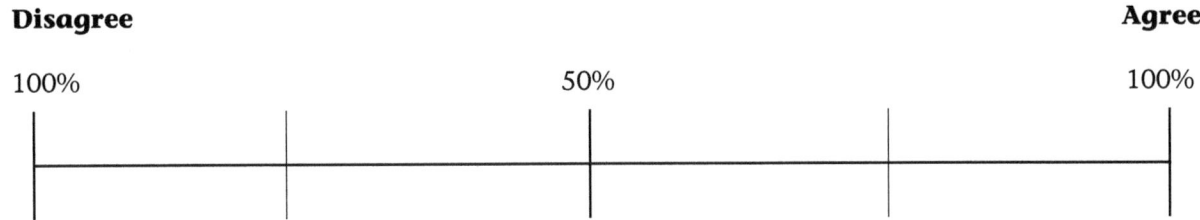

3) For each issue, explain why you put the item where you did. What parts of the topics or statements do you disagree or agree with?
   Arming Teachers-—Teachers should carry weapons in school to protect students.

   Class Size—Smaller class size is better for students and teachers in the long term.

   No-Zero Grading Policy—Teachers should be able to give a zero as a grade.

Teacher Preparation—The coursework and other requirements for teachers should not change.

Teacher Diversity—School districts' efforts are enough to diversify the teacher workforce.

Teacher Salary—Teacher salaries should be similar to other jobs that have the same degrees.

SECTION III
Teaching and Learning

> **STUDENT VOICES**
>
> "English language arts is much more than literacy tests and whether or not a student can write fast and read faster—it's much more based on how well a student can think outside the box and make connections and personal relationships with the text and their own identities."

Chapters

7 Pedagogy and Learning Environments   113
8 Curriculum and Assessment   123

Current Issues and Trends to Be Explored

Common Core
Common Curriculum
English Language Learner (ELL)/Bilingual Education
Standardized Testing
Student Accommodations

CHAPTER 7
Pedagogy and Learning Environments

> **STUDENT VOICES**
>
> "Students would have to be very respectful of each other and motivated to learn and work together. They would also need to be comfortable with each other to be able to openly discuss the content. I imagine this would be difficult for shy kids, but after a while I think they would get used to it and benefit from the communication."

Vocabulary

Accommodation
Bilingual Education
Classroom Climate
Departmentalized
English Language Learner (ELL)
Learning Environment
Prep Periods
Print-Rich
Self-Contained
Team Teaching

Objectives

1. Communicate effectively with educational terms
2. Interpret data presented in graphs and charts about the field of education
5. Explore the role of schools in maintaining, perpetuating, and influencing culture, both nationally and internationally
6. Develop knowledgeable, reflective, and critical perspectives of education
7. Debate current standards, requirements, and trends in early childhood through secondary education

Teaching Methods

Educational philosophies help define *why* teachers teach, design assignments, and arrange their classrooms the way they do. Teaching methods help define *how* teachers do what they do.

Figure 7.1 Common Teaching Methods

Common Teaching Methods		
Discussion	Games	Field trips
Lecture	Research	Think-pair-share
Experiments	Question and answer	Role play
Graphic organizers	Group work	Reflection
Visual aids	Notetaking	Projects
Observation	Multimedia	Guest speakers
"Do now" activities	Presentations	Rubrics
Journals	Hands on/manipulatives	Writing
Artifacts	Primary Sources	Secondary Sources

Source: April Graziano

113

Teachers use many different teaching methods (Figure 7.1) depending on what they are teaching, who they are teaching, what their students need, and what teaching resources and space they have (Figure 7.2). As mentioned in Chapter 3, teaching requires teachers to creatively draw on their knowledge to make numerous decisions before, during, and after teaching. As teachers gain a wealth of knowledge and experience, they are able to adjust their teaching methods as students' needs change, as new data is gathered, and as new learning goals are set.

Figure 7.2 Selecting and Adjusting Teaching Methods

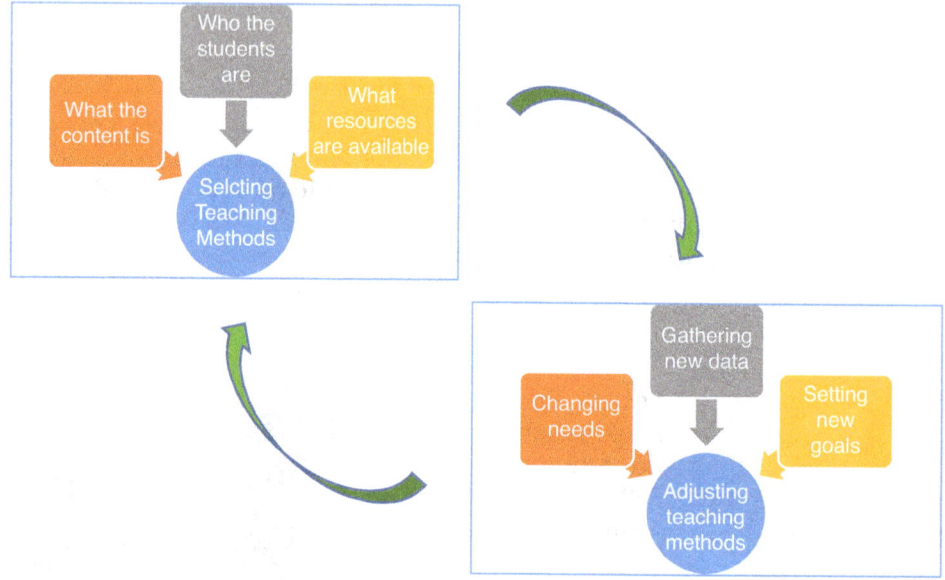

Source: April Graziano

Classroom Climate

Classroom climate refers to the atmosphere in a classroom—how people feel in the room, how they interact, and how they solve problems and help each other. It also includes what teachers and students expect from themselves and others.

Teaching methods can support respectful and collaborative classroom climates where teaching is effective and learning is fun. But teachers need to be flexible leaders so they can change teaching methods when something goes wrong. In addition, they need to use multiple approaches to present information in several different ways and help students learn.

Classroom climate–The attitudes and behaviors of people in a classroom that make the room feel either welcoming or uninviting

> **STUDENT VOICES**
>
> "One thing that surprised me was that students could handle the responsibility of learning alone or with other peers and being in charge. It seemed like being in charge of classes gave them motivation to participate and learn the material more. What inspired me was how well this seemed to work and how good it would have been if I was in class and had that style of teaching. Often I found myself ahead of the rest in math and science but severely behind in reading and writing. Feeling already behind in a subject I was bad at made me just want to give up on it even more and dislike it. But in this system everyone learns on their level and that seems really productive to me".

Supporting Student Learning

One way teachers effectively support students is by planning different tasks for different segments of class. For example, a teacher could have three or four segments during a long class block, which could include five to fifteen minutes each for tasks such as whole group discussion, independent reflection, small group exploration, and sharing of group results. Using segments gives students a break in their physical positions and enables them to switch tasks and remain attentive.

Another approach is providing an agenda for each class. This helps students see the flow of ideas, anticipate the types of activity they will participate in, and gauge the progress of class and time remaining. For students who are strong notetakers, the agenda gives them an overview so they can anticipate the type of notes they'll need during class. For weaker notetakers, the agenda provides a general outline to help them organize the ideas discussed in class.

Using visuals, multimedia resources, and active engagement are other ways to support student learning. Providing information in various formats enables students to look at different aspects of an idea and to use a variety of sensory inputs to aid memory. Active engagement helps students experience learning and helps them recall information because they are emotionally involved in their learning. It also gives students a low-risk way to participate in class. They can use physical and social skills instead of just verbal skills in their learning.

Quick teaching approaches for the beginning and end of each class can help strengthen student comprehension. Teachers sometimes begin class with a "Do Now" activity, a brief activity before the lesson begins that reviews an idea from homework or the previous class. This type of activity before the lesson can also activate prior knowledge, helping the students think about what they already know about a topic they will study. Ending class with a brief question for reflective writing helps students remember what they learned during class, and rereading the journals later gives students a way to look back at their own learning. These strategies only take a few minutes each, but they can make a big difference in helping students remember and respond to what they learn, which makes it easier for them to understand what they learn.

MEDIA EXTENSION FEATURE

Student Centered Learning (5:47)

https://www.youtube.com/watch?v=kbhzhCkI85c

Student Centered Learning—In the Upper School

https://www.youtube.com/watch?v=nfOd6WRPg3Y (4:12)

STUDENT VOICES

"This type of education program seems to be very realistic in terms of teaching. It is able to meet the students at their capabilities and be honest with where they are in their learning."

Student Accommodations

Students who have exceptional learning or physical needs might need special support for learning or moving around the school. **Accommodations** are made when needed to help all students have access to quality education. Students who have suffered trauma or other high levels of stress might need accommodations such as time to rest or remain calm without noise. Sometimes the accommodations are long term, and sometimes they help with a temporary situation like an injury from an accident.

Accommodations are also needed when a student is an English language learner (**ELL**), a student whose first language is not English. In order for ELL students to learn in most American schools, they need to have language

Accommodations– Special support for students for long-term or temporary help due to learning, physical, behavioral, or other needs

learning support. Participating in **bilingual** education (with two languages) can support students who need to learn English by putting them in a class where their native language is spoken and there are other students who are also learning English. Bilingual programs can range from full day in a special language classroom to a full day in an English classroom. Teachers and administrators must work hard to make sure that all students have access to education, and that all students can learn regardless of their backgrounds and prior learning.

Learning Environments

The physical spaces and resources for teaching and learning make up the **learning environment**. Examples of learning environments include childcare centers; school classrooms, playgrounds, gyms, and other areas; libraries; and community centers. These areas need to include age-appropriate resources to help the students learn and to help the teachers and other educators meet student needs. Classrooms also need to be **print-rich** environments without being overwhelming, having words around the room to help students increase their vocabulary (word cards on objects) and for student reference (word wall of recent vocabulary). For online classes, the learning environment includes the learning platform (Google Classroom, Moodle, Blackboard, etc.) where the teaching resources, discussion forums, and other learning activities take place.

Traditional teaching methods tend to take place in learning environments that are teacher-centered with the teacher's desk in the front or center of the room and with students sitting in rows. Progressive teaching methods tend to take place in student-centered learning environments with students working together in groups, with various seating options and activity areas for students, and with the teacher's desk on the side or in the back (Figure 7.3).

As we discussed in Chapter 1, almost all teachers use a combination of multiple approaches. Teachers often begin a new school year with more traditional, teacher-centered pedagogy to help students understand expectations for behavior and performance. Then they can begin using more progressive, student-centered pedagogy as students show that they can be respectful of the teacher and each other when they are given more independent tasks. In addition, if a class starts to have behavior issues, teachers can rearrange desks and temporarily return to teacher-centered pedagogical approaches until the students can regulate their behavior and properly handle responsibility for their own learning.

Furniture arrangements and traffic patterns within the room contribute to the classroom climate and the types of activities a teacher can use. Keep in mind, though, that some classrooms are shared by multiple teachers. In shared rooms or rooms with very limited space, teachers might not be able to move furniture into more student-centered arrangements.

Figure 7.3 Examples of Traditional and Progressive Classrooms

Traditional Classroom
Teacher-centered
Desks in rows

Progressive Classroom
Student-centered
Small groups

Self-Contained Classrooms

Many elementary classrooms are **self-contained** classrooms. One teacher and one group of students work together for the whole school day and for most or all subjects. Elementary licenses are usually for a grade range such as 1 to 6, meaning an elementary teacher can teach any of the grades and curriculum areas for those grades. Classroom teachers tend to teach all subjects for a specific grade. Elementary schools often hire other elementary teachers to teach special focus areas such as physical education or an extra science class. These teachers typically do not have classrooms because they travel to different rooms to teach a class block while the classroom teachers have **prep periods**, time to prepare their lessons and materials.

> Self-contained–Standing alone
>
> Prep period–Time block during the school day/week to prepare lessons and materials

Departmentalized Classrooms

Most high school teachers teach in **departmentalized** classrooms. A teacher has an assigned room and, except for a homeroom group for attendance, they teach different groups of students each class period. Students travel throughout the day to different teachers who only teach a single subject such as English or music. Teachers might teach multiple levels of the same subject (algebra, honors algebra) or different topics in one subject area (US history, world history), but they teach in specific curriculum areas for which they are licensed.

Team Teaching

Middle school and junior high school teachers tend to have departmentalized classrooms, but unlike high school teachers they are often grouped into teaching teams. This allows students to switch from room to room for different subjects, but their teachers work together to get to know the students and help meet their needs. **Team teaching** can be used at other levels, but when it is used for middle school and junior high, it provides a transitional approach for students as they prepare for being more independent in high school.

> **Departmentalized**–Set aside for a single department (or subject area)
>
> **Team teaching**–Teachers who have their own rooms but work together with the same group of students

Unique Learning Environments

There are many other types of learning environments, some of which are very unique in their content focus (magnet school for fine arts), in their scheduling (vocational schools with different weeks for class and shop), or locations. One example of a learning environment with an unusual location is an internship, which gives students the opportunity to spend part of the school day in a workplace for on-the-job training. Another example is a forest kindergarten. This learning environment is discussed with five model programs in the following media extension feature:

MEDIA EXTENSION FEATURE

Forest Kindergartens

Some kindergarten and preschool programs are held outdoors for all or part of the day so children can spend time learning through play in the woods or fields, free to move around instead of remaining seated in a classroom. These programs are called forest kindergartens, and they range from one day per week outside and four days inside, to the full day and full year outside with no building. They are not uncommon in countries like Switzerland and Denmark, and there are a few areas of the United States that have forest kindergartens or other outdoor learning environments.

Switzerland—School's Out: Lessons from a Forest Kindergarten (trailer, 3 minutes) *Scroll down to the trailer.* Children spend all day, all year outdoors with no building. http://www.schoolsoutfilm.com/DVD.php (The full documentary is astonishing.)

Denmark—Kids Gone Wild: Denmark's Forest Kindergartens (12 minutes) *Scroll down to video.* Kids spend almost all their time outdoors. https://wildaboutdenmark.com/whats-the-thing-about-danish-forest-kindergartens/

Canada—The Rise of Forest Kindergartens (news feature, 6 minutes) There are full-time and part-time groups that spend the majority of their time outdoors. https://www.youtube.com/watch?v=g3QwHJmUvBg

Vermont—Best Day Ever: Forest Kindergartens in VT (16 minutes) Students spend one day per week in the forest and the other days in their school. https://www.youtube.com/watch?v=1pC2hAvVn-c

Tennessee—Nature's Classroom: Forest Kindergartens in the Tennessee Valley (10 minutes) A private kindergarten is almost all outdoors. Public schools spend one day per week outdoors. https://www.youtube.com/watch?v=0r__q3VNq9o

> **STUDENT VOICES**
>
> "I think Forest Kindergartens should be a lot more common than they are and I would love to see an increase of forest classrooms in the future. From the videos, I have learned that an outdoor education is very beneficial in many ways. For one, students learn how to regulate themselves and know their own personal limits. It teaches them to measure the risks of their actions and to make decisions for themselves. It also gets the students excited about learning and allows them to take ownership of their education, which hopefully instills a love of learning in them forever. I think it is essential that humans get back into nature because there is so much data that shows the mental and physical benefits."

Field Experience Documentation Form

COLLEGE COURSE

College:
Course Number and Name:
Professor's Name:
Number of Required Hours:

COLLEGE STUDENT

Student's Name:
Student's College Email:
Student's Major:

OBSERVATION SITE

School or Center Name:
Address:
Phone Number:
Name of Principal or Director:
Name of Teacher(s) Observed:
Grade(s) or Subject Area(s) Observed:

OBSERVATIONS

Dates	Times	Number of Hours
	TOTAL HOURS	

SIGNATURES AND DATES

Teacher(s) Observed:	
Student	
Professor:	

Field Experience Paper 2

Name: _____ Due date: _____

Total length required: Other requirements:

Respecting Confidentiality: Please be respectful of the teachers and children that you observe. Unless you have their permission, do not use their actual names in your papers. For teachers, you can abbreviate their names. For children, you can use a first name, but don't use a full name.

Answer the following questions in paper format without question numbers:

1. Where are you observing, and how many observation hours have you completed as of the date of this paper? (Write a paragraph of two or more sentences. Be sure to state the setting you are observing: public/private, school/afterschool/childcare, age/grade/subject.)
   For questions two to five, write a paragraph of three or more sentences to answer each question.
2. Describe the school community members that you met or observed. (Who are the members of the school or center? What are their responsibilities?)
3. Describe how someone (the teacher, you, a student, etc.) helped a student during your time at the school or center. Where was the student, what did he or she need, and how was someone able to help him or her?
4. What have you learned about **students** from observing in this setting? (Student learning, student needs, learning styles, behaviors, other issues, etc.)
5. Is this an age group or subject area that you would enjoy teaching? Why or why not?

_____
_____
_____
_____
_____
_____
_____
_____
_____
_____
_____
_____
_____
_____

CHAPTER 8
Curriculum and Assessment

> **STUDENT VOICES**
>
> "Knowing exactly what a student needs is crucial in helping them learn the material. It allows students who have similar learning styles to be taught together or to help each other as peers."

Vocabulary

Common core
Common curriculum
Failing schools
Learning standard
Learning target
Standardized testing
Student mobility
Turnaround plan

Objectives

1. Communicate effectively with educational terms
3. Explore the nature and value of education in society
4. Demonstrate an understanding of education from historical, philosophical, social, and political frameworks
5. Explore the role of schools in maintaining, perpetuating, and influencing culture, both nationally and internationally
6. Develop knowledgeable, reflective, and critical perspectives of education
7. Debate current standards, requirements, and trends in early childhood through secondary education

Common Curriculum

State department of educations (DOEs) outline what students need to learn in each grade, and school districts select curriculum resources for teaching each grade. This enables each state to select its own goals and expectations for learning. However, different curricula (plural of curriculum) in different states can also cause disparity between what students in one school district or state learn and what students in another location learn. It can also cause issues because of **student mobility**, when a student moves from one district to another. If something is taught at different times or in different grades, the student will miss learning content. Since learning about a topic builds on prior learning, missing content can have strong impacts on student success.

Student mobility– Changing schools or school districts due to a move or change of housing across states or even just changing neighborhoods

Common curriculum is a concept that every district in the country would have the same curriculum, so that a fifth-grade student in Wyoming would learn about the same content as a fifth-grade student in Hawaii, Puerto Rico, or the District of Columbia. The federal DOE cannot regulate a common curriculum because the state DOEs have the authority to decide what will be taught in their schools. Although there are educators who support the concept of a common curriculum, deciding to actually adopt a common curriculum would be a very challenging task since each location would naturally prefer its own current curriculum instead of a common curriculum proposed by a different state.

Learning Standards

A **learning standard** is a specific piece of information or a specific skill that a student should master in a specific grade level or subject. For example, young children studying plants will be expected to learn the basic parts of a plant (leaf, stem, root, seed, etc.) and that most plants need sun, soil, air, and water to grow. Middle-school students will learn about photosynthesis and how plants convert sunlight to energy. High school biology students will need to master the chemicals that plants use in cellular functions. Learning standards are related to a content area, but they are also specific to grade levels and sometimes specific to the reason the content is being studied. Curriculum standards help measure the quality of teaching and learning.

> **Learning standard**–A specific skill or concept a student should master in a given grade level
>
> **Common Core**–An effort to have all states adopt the same learning standards

Common Core

Another pedagogical concept is the **Common Core**. This is different from the common *curriculum*, which refers to the topics and concepts that would be studied at the same grade levels across the country if it were adopted by all the US states and territories. The Common Core State Standards is an effort to have students master the same concepts and skills as students in the same grade in other states. The curriculum looks at the topics, such as continents, weather patterns, or poetry. The Common Core looks at the detailed *standards* of what the student would learn about those topics to successfully complete each grade.

Learning Targets

Explaining to students what the learning standards and goals are for a lesson helps them focus on what they should be learning. A **learning target** is a technique to help students remember the learning that they are aiming for—what they are trying to learn. One example of how to use a learning target is shown in the Media Extension in this chapter.

STUDENT VOICES

"I think it's great to use ELA as a way to not only teach literacy skills, but to also teach empathic skills when reading and analyzing texts. It's really important for students to recognize conflicts when reading a book or watching a scene, and when students are able to pick out evidence as to why there is a conflict and how it happened, they become much better critical thinkers and capable of great empathetic responsibilities."

> **MEDIA EXTENSION FEATURE**
>
> **Learning Targets**
>
> Using a Learning Target throughout a Lesson
> (Kindergarten, writing a thank you letter)
> https://eleducation.org/resources/using-a-learning-target-throughout-a-lesson (3:10)

Standardized Testing

A typical way to measure what students have learned at a specific grade level is to administer standardized tests. The tests can be efficient ways to gather large amounts of information about each student's learning, but because they are typically high-stakes tests, the stress of taking them can cause students to not perform well and, therefore, not show what they do know.

Although they are stressful and time-consuming, standardized tests are useful because they ask everyone who takes the test to demonstrate the same knowledge and skills. This allows schools and states to measure how well students are doing, and how well teachers are teaching. There are many negatives to standardized tests, but one reason they are still used is because it's hard to see if there are problems in a school or district if there are no measures of student progress.

Measuring Student Learning

There are many ways besides standardized tests to measure student learning. Teachers can observe a variety of learning tasks and look for indicators of learning while students participate in discussions, perform experiments, organize ideas, and create projects. Part of teacher preparation involves not only learning about curriculum and about how people learn, but also how to assess learning in a variety of ways. Teachers need to be able to determine when they need to adjust their lesson plans to meet student needs, and they need to be able to present information in multiple ways to help students learn.

> **STUDENT VOICES**
>
> There is something great about a student being able to teach the information they have learned to another peer. It shows near mastery of the subject, and under this model of learning there could be great success.

Failing Schools

Some schools are called **failing schools** because they have a long history of not preparing students to reach grade level standards. In fact, some schools move students on to the next level of schooling or to graduate even though the students' skills are years below where they should be. These students are sometimes not prepared to succeed in jobs, in college, or as informed citizens.

Holyoke Public Schools (HPS) is one example of a school district that was identified as failing and spent several years addressing specific issues to turn the school district around so that all students succeed. When the state (the Massachusetts Department of Elementary and Secondary Education) decided to designate HPS as a failing school district, it was a very controversial decision. Although some HPS schools were failing, some schools were succeeding.

Declaring the whole district as failing didn't recognize that some schools were doing okay. However, once the state designated HPS as a failing school district, a large amount of funds became available for HPS to make improvements to help all students in all schools succeed. Holyoke made many large improvements because of their efforts, such as a lower high school dropout rate, increased school attendance, and a higher graduation rate. Consider how this issue would affect you as a student, teacher, parent, or community member. NOTE: Failing schools was a central issue in the documentary, Waiting for Superman, which is in a Media Extension feature in Chapter 2.

Failing schools– Schools that historically have produced students who fail to meet performance standards

Turnaround Plans

Turnaround plans are outlined steps that a failing school or district will take to interrupt a cycle of failing and make meaningful changes to school performance. In Massachusetts, there are five levels for school designations. Level 1 identifies schools at the highest level of success, and Level 2 identifies a school that is largely successful. Level 3 indicates that a school has some successful aspects, but has many other areas that need to be worked on. Schools in this group could become failing schools if problems increase. Level 4 indicates that a school is failing and needs to make strategic changes immediately to address specific areas of need. If a school in Level 4 does not improve within a given time period, it will be designated a Level 5 school and the state will take over the school.

Turnaround plans outline what a school's administrators, teachers, parents, and community will do to address specific problems so that a failing school becomes a successful school. In Massachusetts, there are four turnaround practices, which are based on research and help schools focus their improvement efforts:

- Leadership, Shared Responsibility, and Professional Collaboration
- Intentional Practices for Improving Instruction
- Student-Specific Supports and Instruction to All Students
- School Climate and Culture

> **STUDENT VOICES**
>
> "I think the idea to embed learning targets and lessons with meaningful projects that the students care about is a great way to teach students classroom skills. It's really easy to teach students if they are actually *interested* in the learning process!"

Chapter 8: Curriculum and Assessment   127

Reflective Writing

Name _____   Due date _____

Required length:

Other requirements:

Directions:

1. Select one of the photographs from Chapter 8 to write about aspects of curriculum and assessment. Which picture did you choose? Circle the letter of your answer.
   A. Chalkboard with "idea" written everywhere
   B. Chalkboard with "A teacher takes a hand . . ."
   C. Student focused on organizing information
   D. Light bulb with a graduation cap

2. Brainstorm at least 10 words or phrases that you think of when you see the photo.

3. **Describe how the image is related to curriculum and assessment.** You can use one of the following questions or use another approach in your writing, and you can use the back of this page if you need more room.
   A. What do you like or dislike about the photo? Why?
   B. Would you change this photo in any way? Why?

Name _____   Due date _____

Section III – Issues and Trends in Education

Directions

1) Consider the educational issues and trends that were discussed in Section III. Think about the arguments related to each issue, and then show how much you disagree or agree by placing that issue on the following line:

   Common Core—States should be able to set their own learning standards for their students.
   Common Curriculum—There should be a national curriculum that is the same in every state.
   English Language Learner (ELL)/Bilingual Education—ELLs do not need support in the classroom.
   Standardized Testing—Although it is stressful, standardized testing is the best assessment.
   Student Accommodations—With proper accommodations, all students can fully succeed.

2) Place a dot on the diagram for each item and label the items.

Disagree   **Agree**
100%   50%   100%

|—————————|—————————|—————————|—————————|

3) For each issue, explain why you put the item where you did. What parts of the topics or statements do you disagree or agree with?

   Common Core—States should be able to set their own learning standards for their students.

   Common Curriculum—There should be a national curriculum that is the same in every state.

   ELL/Bilingual Education—ELLs do not need support in the classroom.

Standardized Testing—Although it is stressful, standardized testing is the best assessment.

Student Accommodations—With proper accommodations, all students can fully succeed.

APPENDICES

Appendix I
    Bibliography   133

Appendix II
    Additional Field Experience Forms   135

Appendix III
    Additional Worksheets and Assignments   145

APPENDIX I
Bibliography

Adichie, Chimamanda Ngozi. "The Danger of a Single Story." *TED Talk*, October 7. Accessed March 15, 2020. www.youtube.com/watch?v=D9Ihs241zeg.

Anthony, Rebecca, and Coghill-Behrends, W. 2014. *Getting Hired*. Dubuque, IA: Kendall Hunt.

Grant, David. "Using a Learning Target throughout a Lesson." *EL Education*, 2011. Accessed March 15, 2020. eleducation.org/resources/using-a-learning-target-throughout-a-lesson.

Hardee, Chris. "Best Day Ever: Forest Kindergartens in VT." Accessed March 20, 2020. www.youtube.com/watch?v=1pC2hAvVn-c.

"Kids Gone Wild: Denmark's Forest Kindergartens." 2020. Accessed March 20, 2020. wildaboutdenmark.com/whats-the-thing-about-danish-forest-kindergartens/.

Koonce, Glenn L. 2017. *Taking Sides: Clashing Views on Educational Issues*. 19th ed. McGraw Hill.

Massachusetts Department of Elementary & Secondary Education. "Culturally Responsive and Sustaining Schools and Classrooms." Accessed March 15, 2020. www.doe.mass.edu/odl/e-learning/culturally-resp-sust/content/index.html#.

Massachusetts Department of Elementary & Secondary Education. "Student Centered Learning." Accessed March 15, 2020. www.youtube.com/watch?v=kbhzhCkI85c.

Massachusetts Department of Elementary & Secondary Education. "Student Centered Learning-In the Upper School." Accessed March 15, 2020. www.youtube.com/watch?v=nfOd6WRPg3Y.

Massachusetts Department of Elementary & Secondary Education. "The Value of Teacher Leadership." September 3. Accessed June 1, 2020. www.youtube.com/watch?v=tMLIZHe0lEk&feature=youtu.be.

Massachusetts Department of Elementary & Secondary Education. "What Do Data and Research Tell Us about Student and Teacher Diversity in Massachusetts." *[Flyer]*. March 2019.

Molomot, Lisa. "School's Out: Lessons from a Forest Kindergarten." [trailer]. 2020. Accessed March 20, 2020. www.schoolsoutfilm.com/DVD.php.

National Association of State Directors of Teacher Education and Certification (NASDTEC). "Table 234.50. Required Testing for Initial Certification of Elementary and Secondary School Teachers, by type of Assessment and State: 2015 and 2016." *NASDTEC Knowledgebase*, April. Accessed May 8, 2020. www.nasdtec.net/.

National Center for Education Statistics. "Estimates of School Statistics, selected years, 1969-70 through 2016-17." August. Accessed May 8, 2020. nces.ed.gov/programs/digest/d17/tables/dt17_211.60.asp.

Pugh, Tyler. Ed. "Nature's Classroom: Forest Kindergartens in the Tennessee Valley." June 9. Accessed March 20, 2020. www.youtube.com/watch?v=Or__q3VNq9o.

Putnam, Hannah, Michael Hansen, Kate Walsh, and Diana Quintero. "High Hopes and Harsh Realities: The Real Challenges to Building a Diverse Workforce." Brown Center on Education Policy at Brookings, August 2016. Accessed 15 April 2019. www.nctq.org/dmsView/High_Hopes_Harsh_Realities.

Salazar, Ray. "Why I Still Give My Students Zeros." April 4. Accessed February 3, 2020. www.nbpts.org/why-i-still-give-my-students-zeros/.

Social Security Administration. "National Average Wage Indexing Series, 1951-2018." Accessed May 25, 2020. www.ssa.gov/oact/cola/AWI.html.

Taie, Soheyla, and Rebecca Goldring. "Characteristics of Public and Private Elementary & Secondary School Teachers in the United States: Results from the 2017-2018 National Teacher and Principal Survey." *National Center for Education Statistics*, August 22. Accessed May 8, 2020. nces.ed.gov/pubsearch/pubsinfo.asp?pubid=2019141.

Teaching and Learning International Survey. "Are Teachers Valued as Professionals?" *Organization for Economic Co-Operation and Development.* Accessed May 8, 2020. www.youtube.com/watch?v=Jc7A3uvAas0.

TeachThought Staff. "How to Create a No-Zero Policy in Your Classroom." January 30. Accessed February 3, 2020. www.teachthought.com/pedagogy/installing-a-no-zero-policy/.

"The Rise of Forest Kindergartens." [news feature]. May 21. Accessed March 20, 2020. www.youtube.com/watch?v=g3QwHJmUvBg.

APPENDIX II
Additional Field Experience Forms

Appendix II—Field Experience Documentation Form.

COLLEGE COURSE
College:
Course Number and Name:
Professor's Name:
Number of Required Hours:

COLLEGE STUDENT
Student's Name:
Student's College Email:
Student's Major:

OBSERVATION SITE
School or Center Name:
Address:

Phone Number:
Name of Principal or Director:
Name of Teacher(s) Observed:
Grade(s) or Subject Area(s) Observed:

OBSERVATIONS		
Dates	Times	Number of Hours
	TOTAL HOURS	
SIGNATURES AND DATES		
Teacher(s) Observed:		
Student		
Professor:		

Appendix II—Field Experience Documentation Form.

COLLEGE COURSE
College:
Course Number and Name:
Professor's Name:
Number of Required Hours:

COLLEGE STUDENT
Student's Name:
Student's College Email:
Student's Major:

OBSERVATION SITE
School or Center Name:
Address:

Phone Number:
Name of Principal or Director:
Name of Teacher(s) Observed:
Grade(s) or Subject Area(s) Observed:

OBSERVATIONS		
Dates	Times	Number of Hours
	TOTAL HOURS	

SIGNATURES AND DATES	
Teacher(s) Observed:	
Student	
Professor:	

… Appendix II: Additional Field Experience Forms 141

Appendix II—Interview

Name _____ Due date _____

Required length:

Other requirements:

Directions:

1. **Getting started**
   Arrange a time to interview an educator, family member, or other community member about the field of education. Here are some ideas to help you get started:

   Educator
   School administrator
   Staff member
   Legislator

   Family member
   Student
   Business owner
   Other community member

2. **Information about the person you interviewed**
   What is the name of the person you interviewed, and how are they involved in education?

   Where did the interview take place?   Date:

3. **Interview questions**
   Prepare some interview questions ahead of time and write them down. You can use the back of this worksheet to create your own questions or take notes.

   A. What type of school did/do you attend, and what was/is it like?

   B. Are there grades or levels of education that are you most familiar with?

   C. What is something that you think is good about education today?

   D. If you could change one thing about American education, what would it be?

   E. Would you recommend a friend or family member to become a teacher? Why/why not?

F. What years of education do you think are the most important for a student?

G. What idea would you want to include if you could design the perfect school?

H. Do you think school funding or teacher salaries should be increased? Why/why not?

I. If you had a favorite teacher in school, what was that teacher like?

4. Write two or more paragraphs to discuss this interview. You can describe how the interview went, things that surprised you, answers that you agreed with or disagreed with, and other ideas to show what you learned about education from this interview.

ns Appendix II: Additional Field Experience Forms** **143**

Appendix II—Interview

Name _____ Due date _____

Required length:

Other requirements:

Directions:

---

1. Getting started
Arrange a time to interview an educator, family member, or other community member about the field of education. Here are some ideas to help you get started:

Educator	Family member
School administrator	Student
Staff member	Business owner
Legislator	Other community member

---

2. Information about the person you interviewed
What is the name of the person you interviewed, and how are they involved in education?

Where did the interview take place?   Date:

---

3. Interview questions
Prepare some interview questions ahead of time and write them down. You can use the back of this worksheet to create your own questions or take notes.

  A. What type of school did/do you attend, and what was/is it like?

  B. Are there grades or levels of education that are you most familiar with?

  C. What is something that you think is good about education today?

  D. If you could change one thing about American education, what would it be?

  E. Would you recommend a friend or family member to become a teacher? Why/why not?

F. What years of education do you think are the most important for a student?

G. What idea would you want to include if you could design the perfect school?

H. Do you think school funding or teacher salaries should be increased? Why/why not?

I. If you had a favorite teacher in school, what was that teacher like?

4. Write two or more paragraphs to discuss this interview. You can describe how the interview went, things that surprised you, answers that you agreed with or disagreed with, and other ideas to show what you learned about education from this interview.

_____

_____

_____

_____

_____

_____

_____

_____

APPENDIX III
Additional Worksheets and Assignments

Venn Diagram Worksheet 147

Issues in Education Worksheet 151

Issues and Trends in Education 157

Name _____ Due date _____

Venn Diagram _____

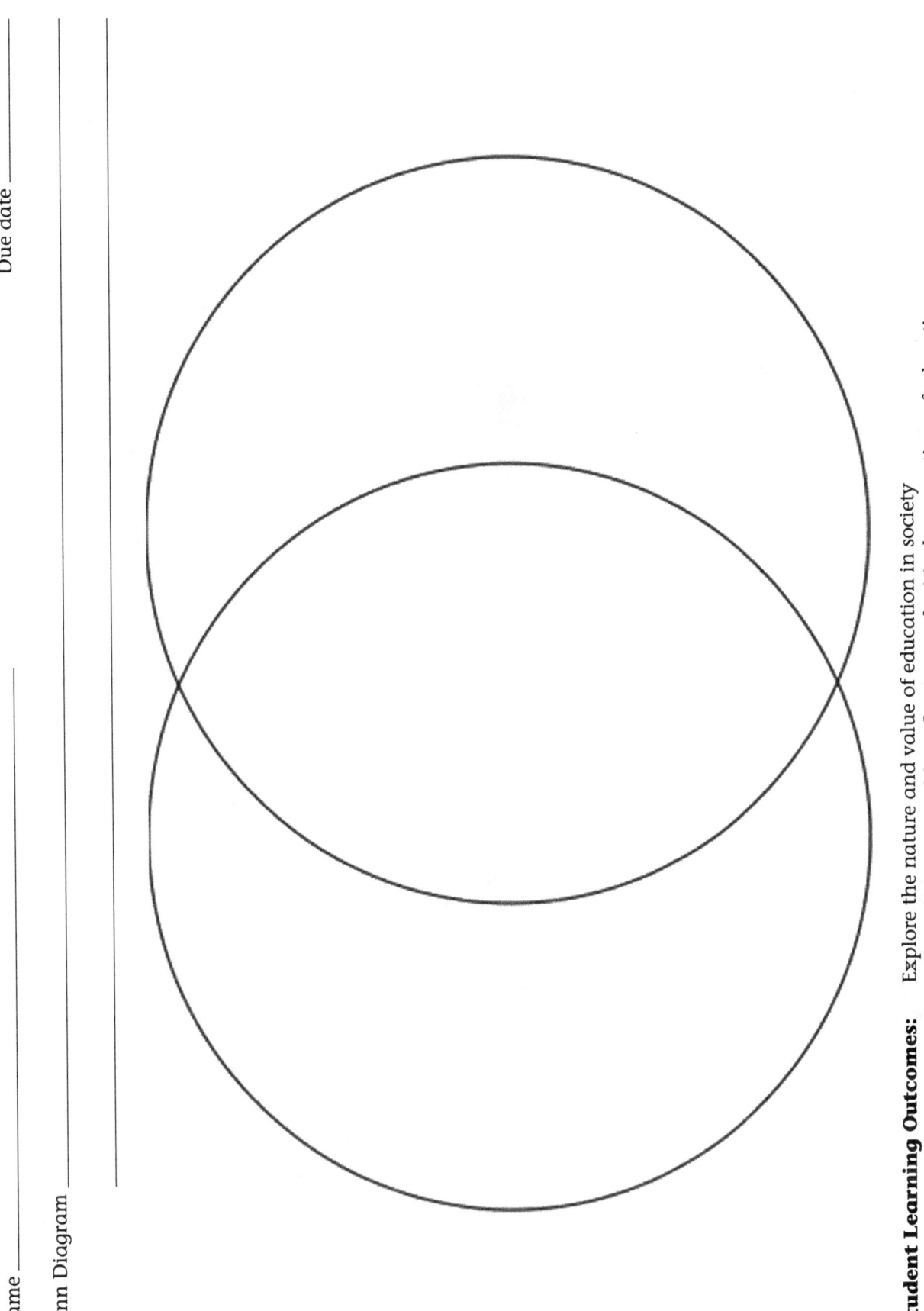

Student Learning Outcomes: Explore the nature and value of education in society
Develop knowledgeable, reflective, and critical perspectives of education

Appendix III: Additional Worksheets and Assignments   147

Appendix III: Additional Worksheets and Assignments **149**

Name _____ Due date _____

Venn Diagram _____

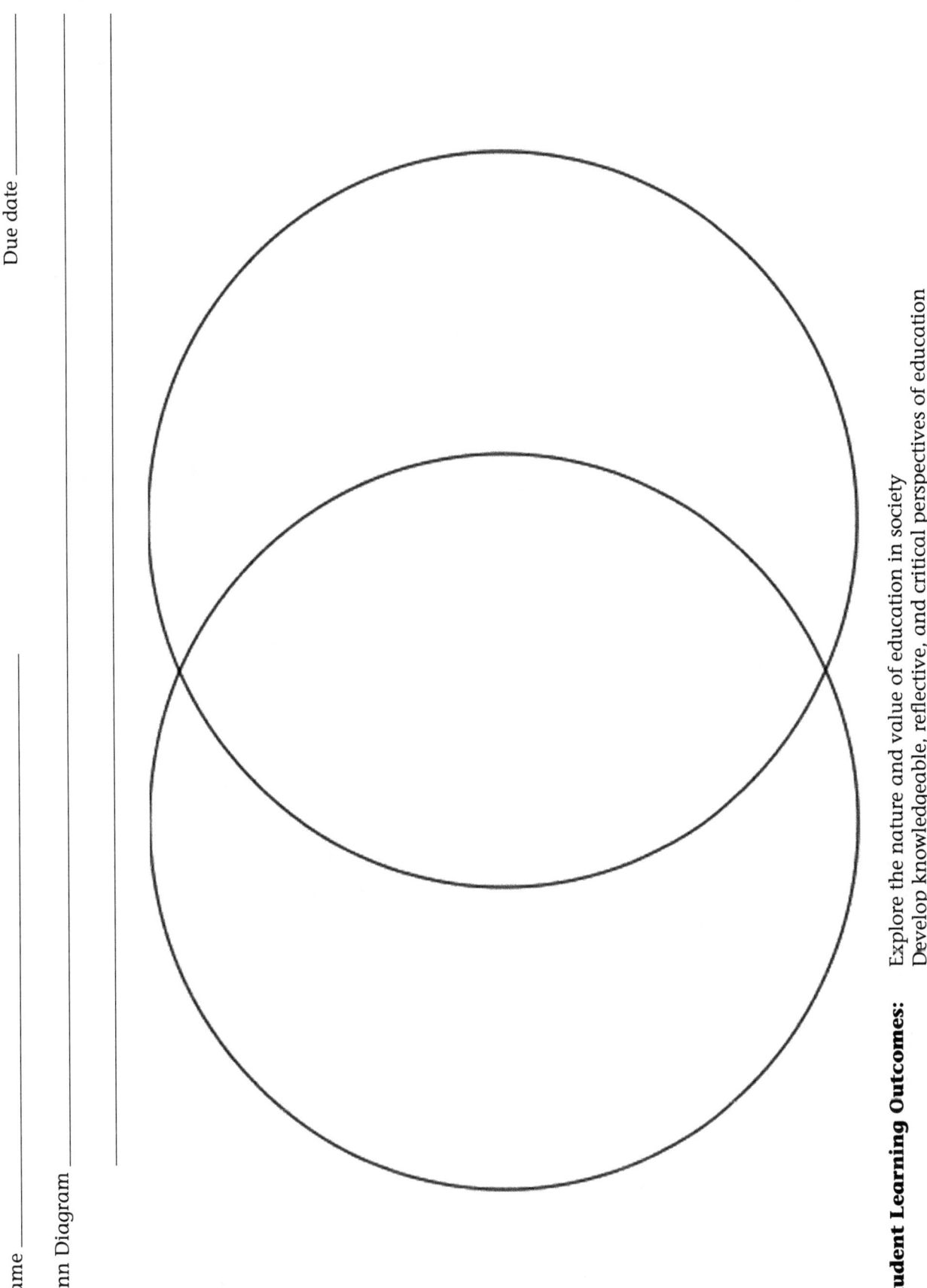

Student Learning Outcomes: Explore the nature and value of education in society
Develop knowledgeable, reflective, and critical perspectives of education

Name _____   Date _____

Issues in Education

What grades/subjects interest you?

Directions
In your small group, discuss current social and/or political issues that impact the grades/subjects you want to teach. Use the following table for note taking, and turn this worksheet as directed.

Issue:		
How does this issue impact teaching, learning, or both?	What solutions could help address this issue?	Other thoughts

Issue:		
How does this issue impact teaching, learning, or both?	What solutions could help address this issue?	Other thoughts

Name _____   Date _____

Issues in Education

What grades/subjects interest you?

Directions
In your small group, discuss current social and/or political issues that impact the grades/subjects you want to teach. Use the following table for note taking, and turn this worksheet as directed.

Issue:		
How does this issue impact teaching, learning, or both?	What solutions could help address this issue?	Other thoughts

Issue:		
How does this issue impact teaching, learning, or both?	What solutions could help address this issue?	Other thoughts

Name _____   Date _____

Issues in Education

What grades/subjects interest you?

Directions

In your small group, discuss current social and/or political issues that impact the grades/subjects you want to teach. Use the following table for note taking, and turn this worksheet as directed.

Issue:		
How does this issue impact teaching, learning, or both?	What solutions could help address this issue?	Other thoughts

Issue:		
How does this issue impact teaching, learning, or both?	What solutions could help address this issue?	Other thoughts

Name _____   Due Date _____

Issues and Trends in Education

Directions

1) Consider the educational issues and trends that were discussed in Education in America. Think about the arguments related to each issue, and then show how much you disagree or agree by placing that issue on the following line:

   -
   -
   -
   -
   -
   -
   -
   -
   -

2) Place a dot on the diagram for each item and label the items.

Disagree   **Agree**

100%   50%   100%

3) For each issue, explain why you put the item where you did. Use the back side for more space. What parts of the topics or statements do you disagree or agree with?

Name _____   Due Date _____

Issues and Trends in Education

Directions

1) Consider the educational issues and trends that were discussed in Education in America. Think about the arguments related to each issue, and then show how much you disagree or agree by placing that issue on the following line:

-
-
-
-
-
-
-
-

2) Place a dot on the diagram for each item and label the items.

Disagree   **Agree**

100%   50%   100%

3) For each issue, explain why you put the item where you did. Use the back side for more space. What parts of the topics or statements do you disagree or agree with?

GLOSSARY

Academic organizations – Provide teachers with current information about academic areas, help them learn from other educators, and help provide professional development for teachers

Accommodations – Special support for students for long-term or temporary help due to learning, physical, behavioral, or other needs

Arming teachers – Giving guns to some or all teachers to help protect students

Autonomy – Ability to work independently

Bachelor's degree – Degree equivalent to about four years of full-time college

Benefit package – Set of benefits that are given to employees

Charter – Permission from a state to begin a new school that is publicly funded but not in a school district, can be independent or part of a charter school network

Class size – Number of students assigned to a class

Classroom climate – The attitudes and behaviors of people in a classroom that make the room feel either welcoming or uninviting

Common Core – Common Core State Standards, an effort to have all states adopt the same learning standards

Common curriculum – Concept that every district in the country would have the same curriculum

Culturally responsive pedagogy – Respectfully representing cultural diversity in pedagogy, content, and resources

Demographics – Characteristics of race/ethnicity, gender, socioeconomics, religion, and so on

Departmentalized – Set aside for a single department (or subject area)

Diversity – Differences within a group—Teacher diversity refers to the different racial and ethnic backgrounds of teachers. Student diversity refers to the racial and ethnic backgrounds of students

Diversity gap – Difference in diversity between two groups

Doctorate – Degree after Master's degree

DOE – Department of education

Educational philosophy – A system of thought about teaching and learning

Educator pipeline – People who are preparing to teach, who are in one of the steps to become teachers

Essentialism – One of two traditional educational philosophies

Existentialism – One of three progressive educational philosophies

Failing schools – Schools that historically have produced students who fail to meet performance standards

Higher ed (higher education) – Refers to colleges and universities

Highly qualified – Having met all requirements for the grade or subject area being taught

Learning standard – Specific skill or concept a student should master in a given grade level

Learning target – Technique to help students remember the learning that they are aiming for—what they are trying to learn

Licensure – Permission to teach, which is awarded for specific areas after all requirements are met

Licensure area – The ages, grades, and/or subject areas that a teacher has met the requirements to teach—for example, elementary (all subjects for grades 1–6) or high school biology (biology for grades 9–12)

Master's – Degree after Bachelor's degree

NCLB – No Child Left Behind Act, the common name for a reauthorization of the federal government's Elementary and Secondary Education Act

NEA – National Education Association

Negotiated agreement – A contract between two groups

Parity – Similar; in regards to teacher diversity, at the same or comparable rates

Pedagogical – Ped/a/gog/i/cal—Related to teaching; for example, a pedagogical method

Pedagogy – Ped/a/go/gy—How and why teachers teach; their skills and creativity

Perennialism – One of two traditional educational philosophies

Policy – A decision made by a governing authority about how something will be done

Prep period – Time block during the school day/week to prepare lessons and materials

Primary school – School that has one or more lower elementary grades such as only kindergarten or PK-2

Progressivism – One of three progressive educational philosophies

PTA – Parent Teacher Association

PTO – Parent Teacher Organization

Reciprocity – Reciprocal (two-way) permission agreed upon by specific states to accept teacher licensure from each other

Rubrics – Tables that list the detailed expectations for an assignment and help determine the value of each part of an assignment

Salary scale – A detailed table that outlines the salaries for people working under that contract

School committee – Also called school board, which is legally responsible for helping to lead the school district

School district – A group of schools from a city, town, or region that share administrators and funding

Self-contained – Standing alone

Social reconstructionism – One of three progressive educational philosophies

Status quo – A Latin term that means the way things are right now, not making changes

Student mobility – Changing schools or school districts due to a move or change of housing across states or even just changing neighborhoods

Student to teacher ratio – The number of students compared to the number of teachers

TALIS – Teaching and Learning International Survey

Teacher candidate – Someone who is in college to become a teacher

Teacher retention – Rate at which teachers are kept (retained) in their teaching jobs, not leaving their positions in a school, district, or state

Teacher workforce – All the people who are teaching in a district, state, or country

Teachers' association – A union for teachers in a school district, state, region, and or country

Team teaching – Teachers who have their own rooms but work together with the same group of students

Tenure – A job security benefit teachers earn after working in a school district, usually after three to five years

Turnaround plan – Steps that a failing school or district will take to interrupt a cycle of failing and make meaningful changes to school performance and help all students succeed

CPSIA information can be obtained
at www.ICGtesting.com
Printed in the USA
LVHW050852290722
724604LV00003B/6